CITY TO THE LICKEYS

A NOSTALIGIC JOURNEY BY BUS AND TRAM

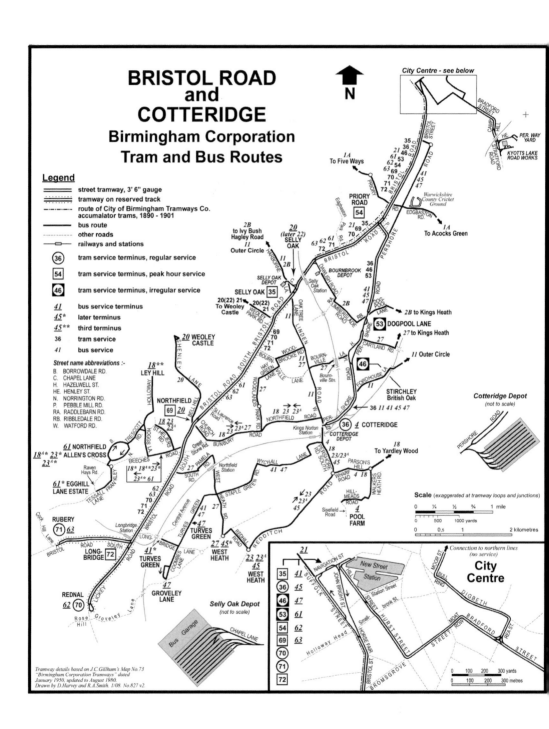

BRISTOL ROAD
and
COTTERIDGE
Birmingham Corporation
Tram and Bus Routes

N

City Centre - see below

Legend

	street tramway, 3' 6" gauge
	tramway on reserved track
	route of City of Birmingham Tramways Co. accumulator trams, 1890 - 1901
	bus route
	other roads
	railways and stations
(36)	tram service terminus, regular service
54	tram service terminus, peak hour service
46	tram service terminus, irregular service
41	bus service terminus
*45**	later terminus
*45***	third terminus
36	tram service
41	bus service

Street name abbreviations :-
B. BORROWDALE RD.
C. CHAPEL LANE
H. HAZELWELL ST.
HE. HENLEY ST.
N. NORRINGTON RD.
P. PEBBLE MILL RD.
RA. RADDLEBARN RD.
RB. RIBBLEDALE RD.
W. WATFORD RD.

Scale (exaggerated at tramway loops and junctions)

0   ¼   ½   ¾   1 mile

0   500   1000 yards

0   0,5   1   2 kilometres

City Centre

New Street Station

Connection to northern lines (no service)

0   100   200   300 yards

0   100   200   300 metres

Selly Oak Depot (not to scale)

Cotteridge Depot (not to scale)

Bus Garage

Tramway details based on J.C.Gillham's Map No.73
"Birmingham Corporation Tramways" dated
January 1950, updated to August 1980.
Drawn by D.Harvey and R.A.Smith. 1/08. No.827 v2.

CITY TO THE LICKEYS

A NOSTALIGIC JOURNEY BY BUS AND TRAM

DAVID HARVEY

TEMPUS

ACKNOWLEDGEMENTS

The author is grateful to the many photographers, both those acknowledged in the text and others unknown, who have contributed to this volume. Special thanks are due to Peter Drake of Birmingham Central Library for his invaluable assistance, Roger Smith for the excellent map and to the proofreading skills of my wife Diana.

First published 2008

The History Press
Cirencester Road, Chalford,
Stroud, Gloucestershire, GL6 8PE
www.thehistorypress.co.uk

British Library Cataloguing in Publication Data.
A catalogue record for this book is available from the British Library.

ISBN 978 0 7524 4697 4

Printed in Great Britain

CONTENTS

INTRODUCTION

There was a time, now coming to the end of living memory, when Birmingham was known as 'the City of 1000 and One Trades' and was the centre of British industry. The range of manufacture in Birmingham was amazing, from pots, pans, kettles and stoves to the most beautiful and delicate jewellery and gold and silverware made in the famous Jewellery Quarter in Hockley. There was the gun industry, brass making, toy, buckle, brooch, pen nib and rope manufacture, printing and there were at least three companies who made billiard tables and cues.

All manner of famous foods had their origins in Birmingham, such as chocolate products made by Cadbury, who pioneered the Garden Suburb concepts of Ebenezer Howard by setting up their factory in the open countryside at Bournville, Bird for custard in Digbeth, Typhoo and Barber for teas and the Midland Vinegar Company of Aston for F. Garton's recipe for HP sauce. Huge companies were based in Birmingham, many of them involved in the 'metal-bashing' trades. Guest, Keen and Nettlefold made nuts, bolts, screws and industrial fastenings, Hoskins and Sewell made bed frames for every type of market and W.T. Avery made weighing machines. In Witton there were two huge industrial companies with Imperial Metal Industries in Witton Road and GEC at the appropriately named Electric Avenue. Dunlop, who pioneered the pneumatic tyre, developed Fort Dunlop, Erdington, in 1916, while in Hockley and Acocks Green Lucas manufactured electrical components.

All this before the car, motorcycle and railway wagon, carriage, locomotive and bus manufacturers have even been mentioned! There were at least twenty car makers based in Birmingham and an amazing total of 105 motorcycle builders. Within the Bristol Road 'corridor', affecting the use and frequency of public transport dealt with in this book, was Ariel Motorcycles in Dale Road, Bournbrook, and from 22 January 1906 'The Austin' moved into the former White & Pike copper plate printing works at Lickey Road, Longbridge. The Austin Motor Co., aka the British Motor Corporation, British Leyland and finally MG Rover occupied a site that was, during the late 1920s, the largest car manufacturing site in the world.

As a result of this industry, the lack of amenities and setting against the appalling living conditions of the back-to-back courtyards and mean terraced housing of inner Birmingham, the 1919 Housing Act was introduced following a pledge by the Lloyd George Government to provide 'homes fit for heroes to live in'. People had a hard life, working all hours for low wages and survived by thrift, community spirit, cheap beer and cigarettes. For many of the men the Saturday afternoon excitement provided by the three large local football clubs of Aston Villa, Birmingham City and West Bromwich Albion was their only entertainment or leisure activity.

Although this book deals with the public transport to Rubery and along Pershore Road it was the 950ft-high Lickey Hills – made up of Pre-Cambrian and Silurian breccias and quartzite – that became the leisure focus for the people of Birmingham. The hills had been made available for recreational use in 1888; the city finally purchased Cofton Hill, Lickey Warren and Pinfield Wood in 1920 and after the Cadbury family purchased the Rose Hill Estate in 1923 and then gave it to the City of Birmingham. It assured free public access to the hills. Summer railway excursions to seaside resorts such as Weston-super-Mare, Blackpool and Rhyl had been available since the 1870s but this was beyond the income of many of the factory workers. From the spring of 1924 until the mid-1950s it was possible to take a trip to the Lickey Hills on the Rednal tram for 5d a ticket and then, for a few years later, by the replacement buses. The only holiday that many people could afford, the hills became the playground for the 'Brummies', with amusement arcades, fairgrounds, bandstands, ice cream parlours and a surprisingly large number of public houses where thirsts could be slaked after a warm day's walking. Until the advent of motorcars and commercial television in the mid-1950s, the Lickey Hills remained an inexpensive and enjoyable day out. It was the increased accessibility to the coastal resorts for a cheap week's holiday that effectively began the decline of the Rednal area just into the era of the new buses which had replaced the tramcars in 1952.

Today there is not much left at Rednal, save for an amusement arcade and a couple of public houses. The Lickey Hills Country Park still provides walks through the hills and the excellent Visitor Centre provides information, guided tours and refreshments.

Now take a journey along Bristol Road and Pershore Road from the city centre to Rednal and Rubery and to Cotteridge by tram and bus. Look at the street scenes from a different time and see why the Lickey Hills became such an attraction.

Horse buses, horse trams and accumulator trams

The first local public transport to travel along Bristol Road was a horse bus service from Snow Hill via High Street, Worcester Street, Smallbrook Street and along Bristol Road as far as the first turnpike gate in Edgbaston. This was first operated on 5 May 1834 by one John Smith – you couldn't make it up! For the next forty-plus years there was a local horse bus service from the town centre serving Bournbrook, Selly Oak and even Northfield.

The Birmingham Omnibus Co. eventually took over the operation of the horse omnibus service along Bristol Road in 1870. Most services took half an hour to get to the Gun Barrels in Bournbrook, with some journeys through to Selly Oak and a few as far as the top of Griffin's Hill. The horse bus service was closed on 2 May 1874 and replaced by horse trams using Standard Gauge tracks. These were operated from Saturday 17 June 1876 by the Birmingham Tramways & Omnibus Co., which opened new offices and stables behind the Malt Shovel in Bournbrook. On 24 July 1890 the Birmingham Central Tramways Co. opened a new 3ft 6in gauge tramway whose terminus was in Suffolk Street using twelve forty-eight-seat double-deck battery accumulator trams. The new depot was in Dawlish Road and had 15ft deep foundations in order to accommodate the gantry cradles to hold two trams and their recharging batteries. Although the trams looked similar to the Handsworth cable cars also operated by BCT, problems with leaking acid and maintaining the batteries made the system not totally successful, although they did last in service for almost eleven years.

Electric trams

The City of Birmingham Tramways Co. converted the Bristol Road accumulator tram service on 14 May 1901 and immediately extended it from the terminus at the junction with Dawlish Road, where Bournbrook depot was located, to Chapel Lane, Selly Oak, outside the Plough and Harrow public house. Initially there were fifteen small forty-eight-seater trams built by ER&TCW and numbered 151–165 in the CBT fleet. On 4 February 1902 an anti-clockwise loop was introduced in the city centre taking the trams along John Bright Street into Navigation Street and leaving this terminus by way of Suffolk Street. This was reversed to a clockwise direction on 17 October 1906 when the Ladywood tram service was introduced. The Bristol Road route remained unaltered until 1923 when the outer terminus was moved to the south side of Chapel Lane in Selly Oak.

Meanwhile, on 20 May 1904 a new CBT tram service via Pebble Mill Road to Mayfield Road, Stirchley, was introduced and five weeks later, when the new depot was completed, the route reached Cotteridge on 23 June 1904 using trams from the 189–216 and 239–242 batches of trams. From then the Cotteridge route remained unaltered until closure on 5 July 1952, although the newest class of traditional trams dating from 1928–29, numbered 812–841, were always allocated to Cotteridge along with the two lightweight bogie cars 842 and 843.

The CBT's twenty-one-year lease on the operation of both the Bristol and Pershore Road tram routes was to expire in 1911 and both services were duly taken over by Birmingham Corporation Tramways on 1 July of the same year. By the end of the year some sixty-one trams were taken over by the Corporation from CBT.

It was only after the First World War that further extensions were made to the Bristol Road tram route. On 1 October 1923 the tram route was extended from Selly Oak to Northfield, a distance of some 2½ miles. Soon after, on 17 December 1923, the route was further extended to Longbridge and replaced the original bus services. The introduction of the trams dramatically increased the carrying capacity for the Austin Motor Co.'s workers. Both of the 1923 extensions were made on central reservation tracks except for the street section through the bottleneck at Northfield, and this was only relieved by a by-pass in 2007.

The tram extension to Rednal up the steep hill in Lickey Road was opened on 14 April 1924. The tracks were built on the western side of the road and when a second carriageway was completed in 1939 the existing track became the central reservation. The tramway extension of 1924 enabled mass access to the recently purchased Lickey Hills and made the 8¼-mile tram route the longest in Birmingham. The 200-yard-long terminus loop, cast-iron tram shelters and the ornamental gardens for the new seventy service came into use in 1925 and helped to develop Rednal as the gateway to the new local tourist attraction. On 8 February 1926 a one-mile extension was opened on reserved track from Longbridge along Bristol Road South to the gates of Rubery Hill Hospital as the 71 service. On 12 July 1927 the new Selly Oak depot was opened with an initial capacity of eighty trams and the old CBT depot in Bournbrook was closed. Briefly it had an allocation of buses, but these were soon moved out to the newly opened nearby Harborne garage. Until Tyburn

Road Works was opened in 1929, Selly Oak had the bus body paintshop, while the chassis went to Barford Street garage for overhaul.

It was from about this time that the Bristol Road route became synonymous with high-speed running and in order for this to take place some twenty-five of the 512 class of bogie cars were re-equipped with 70hp motors. In later years 732, and after 1950 762, class air-brake tramcars were used on the two Bristol Road services. Like the Cotteridge route, both Bristol Road tram routes were converted to busses on Saturday 5 July 1952.

Buses

On Bristol Road the first Corporation bus service was introduced in Birmingham. A new tramway feeder bus service was opened from Selly Oak to Rednal on 19 July 1913 using ten Daimler 40hp open-top double-deck buses which served the Austin Motor factory at Longbridge. On 29 November 1913 a further new bus service was introduced to Rubery. This bus service was gradually withdrawn as the 1923 tram extensions to Longbridge were introduced. While the trams were 'Masters of all they Surveyed' on the main arterial Bristol Road routes, bus services increasingly crossed or used part of sections of this main road as they served the ever-developing suburbia in this part of south-west Birmingham.

One of the first was the 1 service from Acocks Green and Moseley which crossed Bristol Road at Priory Road, Edgbaston, and was introduced on 4 October 1914, at which time it was numbered 9. On 8 January 1923, a bus service numbered 10 was introduced between Kings Heath, Cotteridge, Selly Oak and Harborne and crossed Bristol Road at the Oak Tree Lane junction. This route eventually became part of the 25½-mile-long Outer Circle 11 route on 7 April 1926. In Northfield the 18 route, coming from the Green in Kings Norton was introduced on 18 March 1929 and had its first terminus at the Bell Inn in Northfield. On 5 February the following year the service was extended through Northfield's shopping centre and turned off into Cock Lane, soon to be renamed Frankley Beeches Road and reaching a new terminus in Hoggs Lane on the newly built municipal Tinker's Farm Estate. Further alterations took place on 28 June 1933 when both the 18 and the 23 service from West Heath were both extended a short distance to Trescott Road, Allen's Cross.

The new and huge Weoley Castle Estate was a possible contender for tram services but in the event buses were used. A tram feeder service, numbered 20, was begun on 17 October 1930 from Chapel Lane, Selly Oak, and by February October 1935 the service was extended to Navigation Street in the City Centre and on 24 February 1937 six new variations on the 20 route were introduced, of which four passed through Selly Oak. These Weoley Castle routes were operated from Selly Oak garage using a batch of brand new Daimler COG5s, which were by now being ordered in large quantities as the standard pre-war Birmingham bus. On 2 October 1935, Dawlish Road, Bournbrook, became the terminus of a new suburban service from Kings Heath and on 1 January 1939 this route was combined with the 2 route from Handsworth Wood and the Ivy Bush, with the briefly operated through service being numbered 28.

After the service privations and alterations during the Second World War bus-operated Night Services across the city were introduced on 15 April 1946, using either bus or existing tram route numbers. Starting in Colmore Row alongside St Phillip's Cathedral, the NS 69 went to Northfield and the NS 36 terminated at Cotteridge, though the latter was extended to Kings Norton on 22 September 1947.

The abandonment of the Bristol and Pershore Road tram services on 5 July 1952 resulted in a major reorganisation of bus services. Both Selly Oak and Cotteridge garages received a mixture of new JOJ-registered 2901 class MCCW-bodied Guy 'Arab' IVs and 2776 class Daimler CVG6s with Crossley bodies, some of which remained at their original garages for some fourteen years. These new buses were augmented at Selly Oak with exposed radiator Crossley DD42/6s while at Cotteridge twenty GOE-registered Daimler CVG6 were drafted in for the new services. The 36 Cotteridge tram was replaced by a much longer 45 bus service, which went beyond Kings Norton to the Man on the Moon public house on Redditch Road and then on to a terminus at Alvechurch Road. The Rednal and Rubery services were numbered 62 and 63 respectively.

The new 61 bus route to Allen's Cross Estate was introduced, initiating the abandonment of the 23 service. The single-deck 27 route from Kings Heath, by now operated with 1950-built Weymann-bodied Leyland 'Tiger' PS2/1s, was considerably re-routed and used Church Hill to come from Bournville. It then travelled through Northfield before leaving via South Road on Pigeon House Hill to terminate in Alvechurch Road where it shared the terminus with the 45 bus route. 21 July 1957 saw two new bus services. The 21 route followed Bristol Road as far as Weoley Park Road before going via Weoley Castle Estate to Genners Lane, Bangham Pit. The second new service was the 41 route, which after leaving Cotteridge, turned into Camp Lane and went through Staple Lodge to terminate at Culmington Road, Turves Green. On 17 August 1958, the 41 was extended to the back of the Austin Motor Works in Longbridge Lane. A strange anomaly was ended on 28 June 1958 when the NS62 was extended from Northfield to Longbridge Island at the junction with Lickey Road.

A new single-deck bus service from Cotteridge acting as a feeder to the 'main road' Pershore Road services was introduced on 1 December 1963 as the 4 service to Pool Farm Estate. Fifteen days later the 61 route was extended along Tessall Lane to Raven Hays Road. From Northfield another short single-deck operated route was opened on 20 June 1965; this was the 20 which began in Bell Lane and travelled along Shenley Lane to the junction with Gregory Avenue. This route would eventually go into the Weoley Castle Estate. The last new BCT bus route in the area was the 47 which followed the 41 route through Turves Green but continued to a new terminus at Groveley Lane which opened on 2 April 1967.

During the last four months of 1967, Cotteridge received the entire batch of 3681-3730 MCW-bodied Daimler 'Fleetline' CRG6LXs. Finally on 4 February 1968 the Bristol Road and Pershore Road routes left the city terminus in Navigation Street and loaded up in John Bright Street. This was about the same time as Park Royal-bodied Daimler 'Fleetlines' with two-step entrances were delivered to BCT, being also the last single-door buses. The final act of BCT was to convert the Bristol Road services to OMO using 3813-3878 which were two-doored Park Royal 'Fleetlines'.

On 1 October 1969 West Midlands PTE took over from the municipal operation in Birmingham. Selly Oak garage received 3904-3966 which were part of an order for 100 buses, placed by Birmingham City Transport. At 33ft long, with two doors and seating for eighty passengers, they were given appropriately the nickname of 'Jumbos'. These buses were initially quite successful but the pounding they got on the Bristol Road routes led to their premature withdrawal due to structural problems. In 1979 they were replaced by the purchase of eighty second-hand, redundant, former London Transport DMS class Daimler 'Fleetlines' bought at a knock-down price from Ensign of Grays in Essex who modified them for use in the WMPTE fleet. Selly Oak garage's allocation was the first twenty of the batch of these ex-DMS vehicles numbered 5500–5519. In October and November 1979, the first production MCW 'Metrobus' MkIs entered service from Selly Oak and a new era was born. In later years the Bristol Road and Pershore Road routes were operated by Dennis 'Tridents' with Alexander H47/28F bodies.

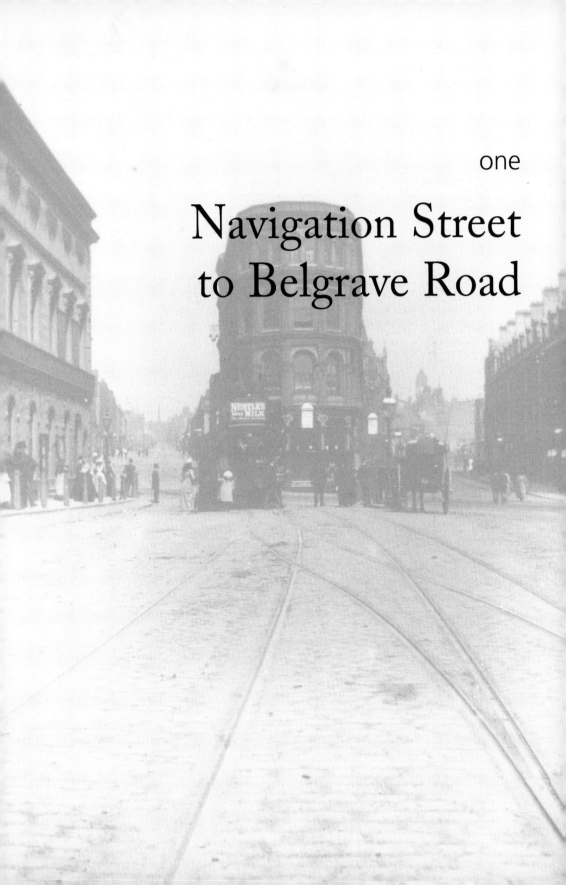

one

Navigation Street
to Belgrave Road

A City of Birmingham Tramways tramcar from the original 151-171 class of 1901 turns out of Navigation Street and hard right into John Bright Street. When CBT opened the overhead electric service to Selly Oak on 14 May 1904 a new city terminus opened in Navigation Street. This formed a loop for the Bristol Road tram service from the Horse Fair–Holloway Head junction into Suffolk Street, Navigation Street and John Bright Street, returning to the Horse Fair. Opposite the turning open-top tramcar is Queen's Drive, a public Right of Way that split the L&NWR side of New Street Station with its impressive 840ft-long by 212ft-wide all-over roof, from the Midland Railway Station. In the distance is the spire of St Martin's parish church in the Bull Ring. (Commercial postcard)

When just five years old 2926 (JOJ 926), a Metro-Cammell-bodied Guy 'Arab' IV, brought into service for the tramway conversion of 5 July 1952, was substantially altered by being fitted with a two-landing staircase which also eliminated the staircase window. This allowed an extra two seats upstairs making it the only fifty-seven-seater in the bus fleet. At the same time the bus was fitted with new Auster pull-in front and side ventilators which considerably altered the appearance of this bus. It is working on the 45B shortworking to Cotteridge and has just left the last group of bus shelters in Navigation Street when turning in front Chetwyn's gentlemen's outfitters into John Bright Street. (F.W.York)

When the 36 tram route to Cotteridge was converted to buses on 5 July 1952, twenty-four-year-old GOE-registered Daimler CVG6s were transferred to Cotteridge bus garage to augment the twenty brand new 2901 class of Guy 'Arab' IVs. 1598, (GOE 598), stands in Navigation Street when working on the 41 route to Turves Green introduced on 21 July 1957 to Culmington Road, just short of Longbridge Lane. As with the trams, the Cotteridge services loaded up at the John Bright Street end while the Bristol Road buses, such as the distant exposed-radiator Crossley, loaded near to the Suffolk Street junction.
(D.R. Harvey collection)

On a sunny day in late June 1952, car 803, a Brush-bodied EMB Burnley bogie air-brake totally enclosed tramcar, waits behind the loading car 833, a Short-bodied Maley & Taunton air-brake car. It is working on the 70 service to Rednal. Car 803 will trundle down Navigation Street to the end stop before loading up to go on to Cotteridge once the Rednal-bound tramcar has left. The distant five-storey late Victorian buildings in Pinfold Street carry the advertisement for the very strong Will's Capstan cigarettes. Opposite the tram stops was the delightful White Swan public house, which was demolished in the late 1960s and the site used for the next thirty years as a temporary car park.
(D.R. Harvey collection)

An unusual tramcar stands in Navigation Street alongside the row of impressive passenger shelters when working on the 35 shortworking to Selly Oak on 29 May 1939. Car 342 was nicknamed 'The Armoured Car' because of its awkwardly styled balcony windows which gave the impression that a Bren gun might suddenly appear from beneath the route number box! 342 had been experimentally fitted with this strangely shaped enclosed balcony in January 1921. This was supposed to be a temporary measure as the Board of Trade would not allow totally enclosed four-wheel trams on narrow-gauge systems. Car 342 and its better-designed 'twin', car 347, survived until the Washwood Heath closures on 1 October 1950. Towering over the tram is the Birmingham Central Technical College, opened by the Duke of Devonshire on 12 December 1895. (L.W. Perkins)

The 'stock-in-trade' buses on the Bristol Road routes for nearly twenty years were the first JOJ-registered batch of 27ft 6in-long Metro-Cammell-bodied Guy 'Arab' IVs. 2950 stands in Navigation Street in about 1958, working on the 63 route to Rubery, while the bus behind is working on the 62 route to Rednal. Navigation Street's road surface, even though it was about six years after the trams had gone, was still mainly covered with stone setts. The buses are parked where there once stood the double-fronted early Victorian Greyhound Inn. (D.R. Harvey collection)

The Limited Stop 99 service was introduced on 3 April 1967 covering the normal 63 service between Navigation Street and Rubery in the morning and evening peak periods. The disadvantage of the Ford R192 for OMO was that passengers had to negotiate the four steps into the saloon and the somewhat intrusive black-painted engine cover that caused a bottleneck at the top of the steps. The driver is issuing tickets from his electrically operated TIM ticket machine, but it was a slow process! The inspector in attendance is supervising the loading of 3652 (JOL 652E), which stands at the 99 bus stop at the Suffolk Street end of Navigation Street on 3 June 1967. (D.R. Harvey collection)

Car 752 turns into Navigation Street from Suffolk Street on 17 May 1952 when working on the 70 route from Rednal. This Brush-bodied sixty-three-seater had EMB maximum traction bogies, Maley air-track and magnetic brakes and was fitted with 63hp DK30/L motors. It had entered service in early 1927 and would be one of the last trams of the 732 class to be broken up in Witton depot during August 1952. The tram is coasting down the gentle gradient in Navigation Street, a parked Austin A40 van visible on the right. In Suffolk Street, passing the sheds of the Central Goods yard, is a speeding Austin A40 Devon. (F. N. Lloyd Jones)

The all-night hourly bus services were introduced on 15 April 1946 and the Bristol Road service was numbered NS 69 and terminated in Northfield. The city centre terminus was in Colmore Row alongside St Phillip's Cathedral, rather than the more out of the way Navigation Street. In 1952 it was renumbered NS62 to match the daytime bus route number and was extended to the Austin factory at Longbridge. Standing in Colmore Row

early one morning, with the Grand Hotel as a backdrop, is 2905 (JOJ 905), a Guy 'Arab' IV 6LW with a Metro-Cammell H30/25R body dating from bus changeover. (F. W. York/R. F. Mack)

No sooner had the decision had been made to bring all bus services as close as possible to the city centre in the 1990s than the scheme to pedestrianise New Street was introduced – in 1999. Leaving only Corporation Street open for service vehicles and buses, the Bristol Road and Pershore Road bus routes had this busy thoroughfare as their city terminus. On 22 November 2003, an Alexander-bodied Dennis 'Trident' 4373 (BV 52 OAL) travels from the distant Old Square and approached the Bull Street junction in Corporation Street. (D.R. Harvey)

Car 816, one of the Short-bodied Maley & Taunton air-brake 63hp trams built in late 1928, spent its whole working life operating from Cotteridge depot. It is about to turn from Suffolk Street into Navigation Street in 1951 when working on the 36 route from the Cotteridge via Pershore Road. The tram is passing the worn-out buildings that included the Suffolk Street premises of West End taxis. Occupying the former CBT waiting room on the corner of Navigation Street is Edward Spicer's taxidermists shop. Behind the tram are a war-time Bedford MWD 15cwt truck and a nearly new Park Royal-bodied Leyland 'Titan PD2/1 coming into the city on the 95 route from Ladywood. (D.R. Harvey collection)

A passenger has just climbed the rear steps of car 102, which stands at the end of the tracks at the terminus of the CBT accumulator tramcar route at the junction in Suffolk Street with Navigation Street. The service to Dawlish Road, Bournbrook, opened on 24 July 1890 and lasted nearly eleven years. This battery tram was built by the Falcon Co. of Loughborough and was 26ft 6in long, sat fifty passengers and had a top speed of 8mph. Behind the six rocker panels on each side of the body were a total of twelve batteries which required recharging twice a day. In front of A. Simpkiss's pawnbrokers and the CBT waiting room on the Navigation Street corner is a recently erected traction pole for the new electric trams to be introduced on 14 April 1901. (Birmingham Central Reference Library)

Car 836, another of Cotteridge depot's thirty Short-bodied air-brake 63hp trams mounted on M&T bogies, climbs up a dingy-looking Suffolk Street on a wet day in 1951. It is passing some very run-down, early Victorian premises and a parked Austin Ten van converted to an estate car by having windows cut into the body side. At the far end of Suffolk Street and towering above the distant tram is the Technical College. (A. Yates)

Picking up passengers outside the Alexandra Theatre in 1946 is Short-bodied lightweight tramcar 842 which is working on the 36 service to Cotteridge. This tram stop was the first one for both the Bristol and Pershore Road services after leaving the Navigation Street terminus and was also shared with the Ladywood 33 route, which took the tracks to the left just behind the speeding motorcycle combination. The devastation caused by the wartime bombing is clearly visible in the gap between the offices in the foreground and the naked gable-end just behind the tram. Overtaking tram 842 is a rather battered Austin Cambridge 10/4 and an earlier Austin 14/6. On the right is Station Street which had been built over the New Inkleys, the worst Victorian slums in Birmingham. (D.R. Harvey collection)

By about 1960 the bottom end of John Bright Street had been swept away as part of the Inner Ring Road Scheme, which was initiated near to this location on 8 March 1957. One of the Cotteridge garage's original bus fleet was 1559 (GOE 559). This MCCW-bodied Daimler CVG6 entered service on 1 November 1947. It is working on the 41D shortworking to West Heath Road and has crossed the remnants of the western end of Station Street and is heading towards the junction of the Horse Fair, Holloway Head and Smallbrook Street. Following 1559 is Guy 'Arab' IV 2957 (JOJ 957), which is working on the 62 route to Rednal. (F.W.York/R.F. Mack)

Looking towards the city centre from the Horse Fair in the mid–1890s, a CBT accumulator car unloads in front of the Malt Shovel public house which occupied the apex of the junction of Suffolk Street to the left and John Bright Street to the right. The pub had been opened in 1883 and was renamed The Argyle in 1903. From this angle the gradient of Suffolk Street can be appreciated. Criticism of these battery trams in their latter years of service concerned the supposed spillage of acid from the batteries particularly onto ladies' long dresses. However, these criticisms were made largely in order to discredit the accumulator cars and expedite the CBT Co. to convert the Bournbrook service to overhead electric cars. On the right is smoke coming from one of the CBT steam trams on its way to Kings Heath. (Birmingham Central Reference Library)

Over thirty years later, in 1929, the scene has hardly altered. The tram going into Suffolk Street is car 357, working into the city on a 70 route service from Rednal. Coming out of John Bright Street is the almost new, totally enclosed bogie car 833 bound for Cotteridge. On the left is the premises of the leather goods manufacturers F.A. Pattison, who had taken over this impressive Victorian block from a paint producing company. On the right with the lanterns hanging above the entrance is the five-storied Bull's Head public house which had been rebuilt in 1912. The policeman is standing in front of The Argyle public house, which closed in 1928. (Birmingham Central Reference Library)

Speeding around the island at Holloway Circus in about 1967 is 2468 (JOJ 468), a 1950 Crossley DD42/6 with a Crossley H30/24R body which was one of fifteen drafted into Selly Oak garage during the previous autumn. The Crossley is working on the 61 route, which terminated in Tessall Lane at the edge of the Egghill Lane Estate, Northfield. This route extension was about half a mile beyond the former terminus at Allen's Cross on 15 December 1963. In the background on Smallbrook Queensway is the fourteen-storey Albany Hotel designed by James A. Roberts, which was completed in 1962 and became the first city centre hotel to be built in Birmingham since the early Edwardian period. (A.A. Turner)

Looking out of the city into the Horse Fair, the steeply gabled St Catherine of Sienna Victorian Gothic church, which had been extended with an enlarged chancel in 1890, towers over the rest of the buildings. The Horse Fair had been renamed in 1812 from its former Brick Kiln Lane and its wideness reflected the regular horse fair which continued until the Edwardian period. In about 1899, one of the CBT accumulator bogie cars from the 101–112 batch stands in the Horse Fair before moving off towards the Suffolk Street terminus. (D.R. Harvey collection)

In the time between the ordering of 100 33ft-long Park Royal-bodied Daimler 'Fleetline' CRG6LXB/33 and their delivery, the operator had changed from BCT to WMPTE. 3959 (SOE 959H) is in the Horse Fair working on 61 service to Egghill Lane Estate in 1971. These double-door eighty-seaters had bodies built to the new Government Bus Grant specification and were nicknamed 'Jumbos' by passengers and staff alike. They were not long-lived buses due to structural body failures and were replaced by second-hand London Transport DMS-class buses purchased in 1979. Behind the bus are the concrete walls of the Bristol Street underpass and the thirty-two-storey Clydesdale Tower, which with its twin, Cleveland Tower, were known as the Sentinels. (J. Carroll)

The CBT converted the battery accumulator bogie trams by tiny overhead electric trams numbered 151–171 on 14 May 1901. These were the first electric trams to operate in Birmingham and were open-top, reverse-staircase trams built by ER&TCW with a forty-eight-seat capacity. Mounted on Peckham 6ft wheelbase trucks they were very hard riding and prone to pitching, so although they were superior to the battery trams in almost every aspect, they gave an uncomfortable ride. The central traction poles in Bristol Street were unique to Birmingham and were replaced before the end of the decade. Bristol Street and the Horse Fair were both busy Edwardian shopping streets. On the left is the tower of St Catherine of Sienna RC church, designed by Dunn & Hansom, which stood on the site from 1875 until 1964. (D.R. Harvey collection)

On the last week of tram operation in July 1952, car 807, a Brush-bodied EMB air-brake tram mounted on EMB maximum traction bogies, travels along Bristol Street going into the city on a 71 service from Rubery. The tram has just passed Wrentham Street, while just beyond car 897 is the Bromsgrove Street junction. On the right is the row of Arts and Crafts-styled buildings with a large Vauxhall Big Six saloon of 1935 and parked outside Mesdames Harman gown shop is an early post-war Austin Eight. (A. Yates)

A number of JOJ-registered Guy 'Arab' IVs were allocated to Selly Oak garage from new in July 1952 until they were replaced by Daimler 'Fleetlines' during 1967. 2953 (JOJ 953) was one of these Metro-Cammell fifty-five-seat buses and is operating on the 41 service in Bristol Street to Turves Green during 1957. These splendid buses were well-suited to the Pershore Road's fast running, though their brakes were prone to fading during hot weather. 2953 is still in more or less original condition as it still had its full-length front wings and trafficators. (R.H.G. Simpson)

The woman with the mink-collared coat pushes a pram along Bristol Street and sees one of the UEC-bodied open-balconied fifty-two-seat trams, mounted on UEC swing-yoke 7ft 6in trucks, travelling along Bristol Street. The tram is working on the 35 route shortworking to Selly Oak in 1933. Car 397, in the smart-looking gold lined-out pre-war livery, had been transferred from Witton depot to Bournbrook in the spring of 1924 when new bogie trams had displaced these four-wheelers. 397 survived in service until September 1949. (J.E. Cull)

While the man tinkers with the side-valve engine of his 1949 Birmingham-registered Ford Anglia E93A a Cotteridge-bound tram travels along Bristol Street during the spring of 1952. Car 837 was one of the 812 class trams Short-bodied 63hp trams of 1929, mounted on M&T bogies that had separate air-wheel brake control, with air-track and magnetic braking available through the main controller. It is passing the showrooms of Bristol Street Motors who are still Ford agents in the twenty-first century. There are a number of Ford cars parked on the pavement, including an almost brand new Consul EOTA and a 1936 Family Ten C Tourer. (F.N. Lloyd Jones)

Travelling out of the city in Bristol Street is UEC-bodied four-wheeled tramcar 307. It is working on the Navigation Street to Selly Oak in about 1915. The tram has flop-over destination boards in the balcony which were only in use between 1908 and about 1915. Beyond the tram, on the far side of St Luke's Road, is the graceful spire of the Wycliffe Baptist church which opened in 1861, while the tall nave of St Luke's church, Bristol Street, is almost where the tram has reached. This Gothic-styled brick church was consecrated in 1903 but never received its intended south-west spire. (Commercial postcard)

The Cinephone cinema, on the corner of Bristol Street and Wrentham Street, replaced an earlier cinema opened in 1912 and known as the Bristol Street cinema. Demolished in 1923, it was then rebuilt as The Broadway before being transformed again in 1956 in a very 'Festival of Britain' style as the Cinephone. It specialised at various times as a news theatre, a cartoon cinema, showing foreign films, but most infamously as showing skin flick films. As one of Cotteridge garage's one-year-old MCW-bodied Daimler 'Fleetline' CRG6LXs, 3706 (KOX706F), passes the cinema on a 45 service in May 1968, the Cinephone is showing *Mondo Bizarre*. The cinema closed on 17 September 1977. (C. Carter)

Car 630 was one of fifty open-balconied bogie trams which entered service in early 1921. It was bodied by Brush with a thirty-four-/twenty-eight-seat seating split and was mounted on Brush-constructed Burnley-style maximum bogies and had BTH GE249A 37hp motors. In June 1923 this tram was equipped with EMB Maley air-brakes and a pair of new EMB Burnley bogies. Ultimately it was fitted with DK 30/1 63hp motors and became the prototype air-brake car. In June 1947 it was transferred from Washwood Heath depot to Selly Oak. It has just crossed the Belgrave Road junction, which is where the Inner Circle 8 bus route crossed Bristol Street. The tram is overtaking a 1936 Staffordshire-registered Morris-Commercial pick-up truck and is being followed by a Hillman Minx Phase III car. (J.H. Taylforth collection)

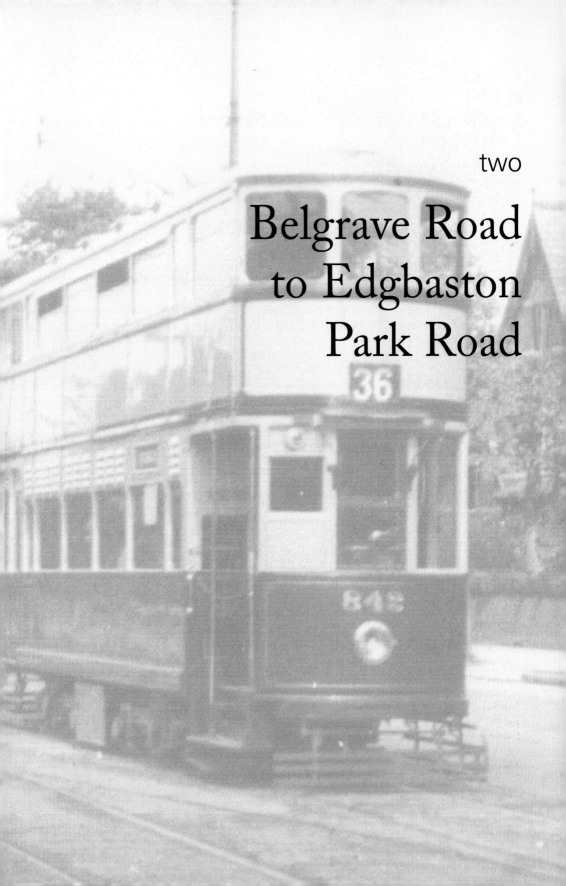

two

Belgrave Road
to Edgbaston
Park Road

UEC-bodied tram 517 had entered service in November 1913 as a vehicle with vestibules, a top deck cover, open balconies and Dick Kerr 40hp motors. During its forty-year service life the balconies had been enclosed, the wooden benches replaced by cushioned seats and fitted with GEC CT 32R 70hp motors. In 1948 it had been heavily strengthened, resulting in the loss of the platform bulkhead window. It is working on the 70 route to Rednal and has just crossed Belgrave Road and will reach Wellington Road at the top of the hill. On the right is the delightful early nineteenth-century Trees pub, formerly a Holden's beer house, which was closed in 1971. On the left is a wartime Austin K3 lorry with a military-type bonnet which is being used in connection with some road repairs. (A.B. Cross)

The Bristol cinema, designed by Hurley Robinson with a capacity of 1,710 people, was neither in the city centre nor in the suburbs, but always showed the big films of the day. It opened on Sunday 16 May 1937 showing *The Luckiest Girl in the World* starring Jane Wyatt. In 1966 it was screening the mediocre 1965 war film *The Battle of the Bulge* with a wonderful starring cast of Henry Fonda, Robert Shaw, Telly Savalas, Robert Ryan, Dana Andrews and Charles Bronson. The Bristol cinema was closed on 24 September 1987 and was demolished within weeks, being replaced by a Drive-Thru McDonalds. The multi-storey flats under construction were pulled down in 2001. A Crossley DD42/6, working on the Inner Circle 8 route, comes out of the as yet unfinished Lee Bank Middleway and crosses Bristol Road. The tall Ottowa Tower stands above the nearby maisonettes while one of Cotteridge's Guy 'Arab' IVs, on a Pershore Road service, picks up passengers in front of Belgrave Road Police Station. (J.Moss)

Selly Oak garage's first Daimler 'Fleetlines' entered service in January 1968. These were Park Royal H43/33F-bodied examples which have the thin pillared front windows that looked as if their designer had got his inspiration from buses built by Christopher Dodson for the 1930s London Pirate operators. 3741 (KOX741F) entered service on 5 February 1968 and is seen soon afterwards passing the Bristol cinema on the corner of the almost completed Lee Bank Middleway, when working on a 62 service from Rednal. Helpfully, the small destination box correctly shows that the bus is going 'TO CITY'. The complex of maisonettes and tower blocks had been replaced by 2007 with houses. (R.F. Mack)

In about 1905, one of the original CBT electric four-wheel trams, car 154, which was later taken over by BCT as car 503, has climbed out of the nearby Bristol Street and is in Bristol Road at the junction with Wellington Road. This was the edge of the Calthorpe Estate developed by Sir Henry Gough, the second baronet, who inherited the Edgbaston Estate in 1774 and died fifteen years later as Lord Calthorpe. By refusing to allow industry beside the nearby Worcester Canal he established the special character of Edgbaston. By 1834 the north-east corner of the parish was already covered with elegant terraces leading to separate houses that were country mansions in all but location. There was development in the Bristol–Wellington–Sir Harry's roads triangle and some of the houses are just visible through the trees on the right. (Commercial postcard)

The development of housing along the inner section of Bristol Road only really began after the end of the Napoleonic Wars. Thus, the very 1930s block of shops with their flats above on the corner of Bristol Road and Wellington Road always looked out of place being surrounded by large and sometimes sumptuous Regency and early Victorian houses. Coming into the city on a 61 service on 28 May 1971 is 3905 (SOE 905H), one of the 33ft-long Park Royal-bodied Daimler 'Fleetlines' which entered service in early October 1969. Parked on the forecourt of the shops on the corner of Wellington Road are a Morris Minor 1000, an Austin A60 Cambridge and an Austin A40 MkII. (Birmingham Central Reference Library)

Bristol Road replaced the meandering roads through Edgbaston in 1771 as the main route to Bournbrook with a tollgate at the Priory Road–Edgbaston Road crossing. It was also the eastern boundary of the Calthorpe Estate and many of the Regency rows and villas still stand. Nos 84 and 86 Bristol Road are typical of the two-storey houses that were built in the 1830s and 1840s, although No.86 has been altered by the addition of a later Victorian bay window. Parked in front of the garage are a 1939 Morris Eight Series E and a 1954 Ford Consul EOTA stands in the Bristol Road carriageway. (Birmingham Central Reference Library)

Although the Gough-Calthorpes were absentee landlords they always maintained their estate in Edgbaston as a 'semi-rural oasis in the heart of an industrial city'. They did this by using restrictive leaseholds that prevent the use of buildings or land for industrial or commercial purposes. Other nearby areas to the early Victorian Birmingham, such as Balsall Heath and Ladywood, became industrialised due to the lack of these restrictions. Edgbaston became a favoured district because although it was so near to the reeking town it was usually free from smoke and smell – thanks to the prevailing south-westerly wind. By 1959, the lovely house on the corner of Bristol Road and Speedwell Road was the consulting rooms for the physician and surgeon Christopher St Johnson. (Birmingham Central Reference Library)

Passing along the tree-lined Bristol Road in Edgbaston towards Priory Road, on its way to Cotteridge in about 1914, is tram 367. This was one of the forty UEC-vestibuled and top-covered fifty-four seaters mounted on 7ft 6in wheelbase swing-yoke trucks that entered service in December 1911. These four-wheelers weighed 12 tons 15 cwt and being low-bridge cars could fit under both Selly Oak and Aston railway bridges. The tram is equipped with flop-over destination boards. At this time the Pershore Road services were being operated from Bournbrook depot as Cotteridge was used as a store. (Commercial postcard)

Bristol Road, Birmingham.

The electricity supply had only been turned off only a few hours earlier when lightweight car 842 had left Cotteridge depot to become the last tram to work along Pershore Road on the Sunday morning of 6 July 1952. A few hours later, travelling into the city is a sparklingly JOJ-registered Guy 'Arab' IV with a Metro-Cammell H30/25R body. 2914 (JOJ 914) was on its first day in service. This bus was one of a total of 225 buses ordered for £1 million on October 1951 to replace the Bristol Road and Cotteridge tram routes. The rear view of the bus shows the large rear fleet numbers that were discontinued during 1953 when small numbers were substituted in order to allow for the positioning of advertisements on the lower rear panelling. (D. Griffiths)

The CBT overhead electric Bristol Road tramway conversion from the battery trams on 14 May 1901 was considered to be most successful. Brush-bodied tram 236 is about to overtake a fashionable female cyclist in this verdant part of Edgbaston near to the junction with Priory Road. This tram was built in late 1904 as one of a batch of fourteen forty-eight-seat trams which ran on 8ft 6in wheelbase Brush-Conaty radial trucks. Yet within three years the original ER&TCW tramcars mounted on 6in wheelbase Peckham 9A cantilever trucks were considered to be too small and excessively rough riding. CBT 236 was taken over by the Corporation in July 1911 and became car 495. It was top-covered and vestibuled during 1924 and survived until January 1937. (Commercial postcard)

Open cab AEC 504, 115 (OM 214), is working on the 1 route from Moseley and is travelling towards the city centre with its driver wearing his weather-proof tarpaulin cape. On 18 August 1925, the bus was about seven months old and is on rubber tyres. It has just crossed Bristol Road and is in Priory Road, Edgbaston. In 1929, Birmingham's first traffic lights were installed at this junction replacing the distant white-coated policeman on point duty. This area of Edgbaston is well known for its tree-lined roads and large Regency and Victorian detached houses such as the example on the right. (Birmingham Central Reference Library)

On 24 September 1979, former London Transport DMS 1277 (JKU 277K), just two months into its new career as WMPTE 5514, enters the yellow box as it crosses the Bristol Road junction with Priory Road travelling into the city on the 63 route. Eighty of these second-hand buses were purchased and twenty of these were allocated to Selly Oak garage to replace the 'Jumbos' that were being prematurely withdrawn due to body failures. The DMS vehicles were rushed into service with the LTE destination boxes only partially painted over, although the centre doors were taken out. (A.B. Cross)

The Selly Oak allocation of JOJ-registered Guy 'Arab' IVs led, by BCT standards, a fairly active life as they pounded Bristol Road on their way to Rednal, Rubery and Allen's Cross for over seventeen years. 2948 (JOJ 948) entered service in October 1952 from Selly Oak garage and is travelling into the city in about 1953 when working on the 62 route from Rednal. It is passing the stone wall which protected the Park Grove house which latterly was part of the Edgbaston College complex and Edgbaston Golf Club. (R.H.G. Simpson)

Birmingham's most modern-looking tramcar was their penultimate one, which entered service in November 1929. This experimental tram was built by Short Bros and was of all-metal construction with aluminium panels, framing and roof. The sixty-three-seater had English Electric bogies, Maley & Taunton air-brakes and a pair of Dick Kerr 40hp motors. At 33ft 6in long, the tram weighed only 13 tons 12¼ cwt, which was some 3 tons 3 cwt lighter than the standard Birmingham tram and was also Birmingham's lowest tramcar at 15ft 6in. In 1938, car 842 draws up to the Bundy Clock at the red plate compulsory tram stop in Bristol Road just before turning left into Pebble Mill Road. (S. Eades)

Thirteen years later, a utility shelter has been added for passengers opposite the Bundy Clock at the beginning of the first section of Bristol Road's reserved track near to the junction with Pebble Mill Road. Brush-bodied air-brake car 772, mounted on EMB Burnley bogies, is manoeuvring across the crossover, enabling it to return towards Selly Oak and on to Rednal as a 70 service on 7 October 1951. Trams going to Priory Road and Pebble Mill Road normally carried the route number 54 when coming from the city. (G.F. Douglas)

Speeding along the tree-lined Bristol Road in Edgbaston with the Pebble Mill Road junction behind it is 2810 (JOJ 810), a Daimler CVG6 with a Crossley H30/25R body, which entered service in July 1952. It is working on the 21 route to the 1960s municipal housing estate Bangham Pit by way of Selly Oak and the huge interwar Weoley Castle municipal housing estate in 1965. (B.W. Ware)

On Thursday 4 June 1931, UEC-bodied four-wheel tram 384 speeds along the reserved track in Bristol Road, Edgbaston, when working on a 69 service to Northfield. This open-balconied tram entered service in January 1912 and by 1931 was one of fifty-nine of the class allocated to Selly Oak depot. The reserved track was about seven years old with the new saplings contrasting with the mature trees which had originally marked the western side of the single-carriageway road. On the right is a McVitie & Price Albion van. (Birmingham Central Reference Library)

After the closure of the Bristol Road routes, all Cotteridge and Selly Oak depots' air-brake trams were withdrawn. Thirty-one trams went to Witton on the Friday before the Bristol Road group closures while the majority of the sixty-two trams sent to the works for storage went on the final afternoon of operation. These latter trams were subsequently taken to Witton, during August 1952, for breaking up by W.T. Bird of Stratford. This left fifty-four withdrawn trams, which were stored on the section of reserved track between Eastern Road and Pebble Mill Road for nearly three weeks. Not one tram was vandalised! Cars 737 and 781 were at the Eastern Road end of this row of trams. These were driven away to Witton for breaking up on 23 July 1952 along with car 513, the last tram to make this journey. (A.N.H. Glover)

Travelling into Birmingham on a 70 service from Rednal is car 776, one of the fifty Brush totally enclosed sixty-three-seaters that entered service in November 1928. It is passing the playing fields of King Edward School at the gap in the reserved track at Eastern Road in June 1952. The 762-811 class trams of 1928 were the first in the fleet to have eight windows in the upper saloon. This was a rather ungainly feature, designed so that each row of seats would be next to an opening window. On this warm day nearly all the windows are open. (D.R. Harvey collection)

On 3 July 1952, a Brush-bodied air-brake tram, car 782, crosses the gap in the Bristol Road central reservation at Eastern Road. It travels towards Pebble Mill Road on an inbound 70 service. The tram is passing the playing fields and grounds of King Edward's School which had moved from the original New Street site in 1935. The temporary wooden buildings were used as classrooms for many years. Behind the school and piecing the distant skyline is the Chamberlain Tower of the University of Birmingham. These EMB air-wheel 63hp cars spent their first twenty-two years operating from Washwood Heath depot equipped with Fischer bow-collectors. Car 776 was transferred to Selly Oak on 30 September 1950. (D.R. Harvey collection)

Above: The Gun Barrels public house was located in Bristol Road on the corner of Edgbaston Park Road. The original building was an eighteenth-century coaching inn and was the last stop for stagecoaches from Worcester on their way into Birmingham. This building was replaced by the six-gabled Victorian public house that became a popular venue for illegal prize fights. As the pub was next to the county boundary that followed Bourn Brook, the pugilists could escape the clutches of the law by simply crossing the river. In later years the Gun Barrels really came into its own as the nearest pub for students at Birmingham University. The pub also had an excellent crown bowling green, which had the rare distinction of being stolen just before the pub was closed on 24 September 1978. A new one was quickly built but the old atmosphere was lost. In April 1925 before the central reservation in the foreground had been built, a distant 301 class car is travelling out of Bournbrook towards the Gun Barrels. (Birmingham Central Reference Library)

Opposite above: Travelling into Birmingham on a 72 service from Longbridge is car 740. This 63hp Brush totally enclosed EMB bogie car is passing Edgbaston Park Road on the left. This road led up the steep hill to the University of Birmingham. The tram is about to enter the soon to be made redundant central reservation while the nearly deserted Bristol Road disappears towards Eastern Road. Parked outside the branch of Lloyds Bank on the left is an Austin A40 Devon. (J.S. Webb)

Opposite below: On 12 April 2003, a five-month-old Alexander-bodied Dennis 'Trident', 4385 (BV 52 OBC), passes the new Gun Barrels Toby Inn on the corner of Edgbaston Park Road. The bus is working on the 62 service to Rednal. On the far corner is the headquarters of the RoSPA road safety organisation and behind the bus is the old tramway central reservation. (D.R. Harvey)

The Birmingham Omnibus Co. took over the operation of the horse omnibus service along Bristol Road from one E. Birch in 1870, with most services going to the Gun Barrels with a few journeys through to Selly Oak and beyond to the top of Griffin's Hill. On the half-hourly daily service the fare to the Gun Barrels was 4*d* inside and 3*d* outside, whereas on the four times daily service to Selly Oak it cost either 6*d* or 4*d* to brave the elements. This fare tariff is written near to the double-doored rear entrance of the splendid tram, though just how the women in their long multi-layered skirts maintained their dignity when climbing the vertical ladder is something of a mystery. The tram appears to be standing near to the Gun Barrels terminus. The horse bus service was closed on 2 May 1874 and replaced by horse trams using Standard Gauge tracks. (D.R. Harvey collection)

Typical of the Birmingham Tramways & Omnibus Co.'s horse trams was car 30, which was built locally by Brown, Marshalls. The standard gauge line was opened on Saturday 17 June 1876 with new offices sand stables behind the Malt Shovel in Bournbrook. The city terminus was in Suffolk Street at the Navigation Street junction. The original intention was to have a cross-town link to the Handsworth horse tramway by going up Suffolk Street but this was never implemented as three horses would have to be employed to get up the steep hill. (R.T. Coxon collection)

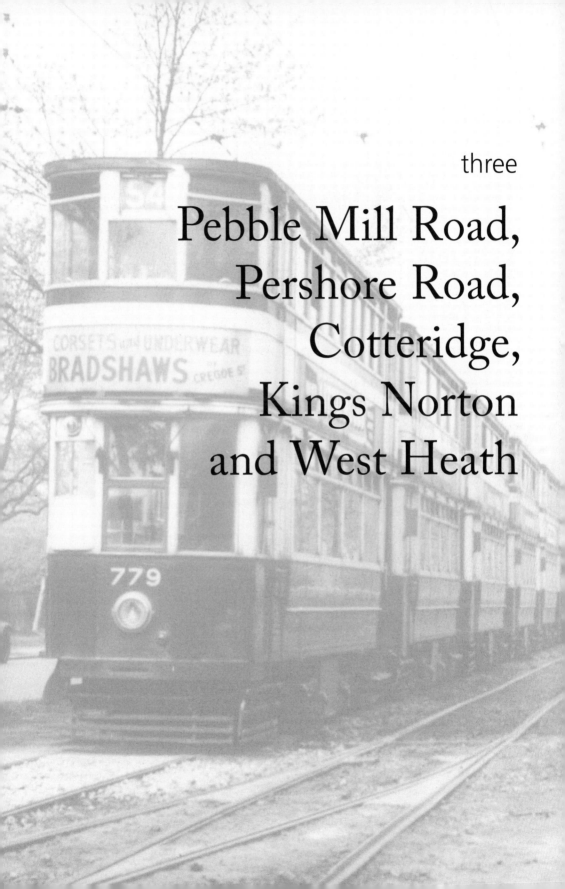

three

Pebble Mill Road, Pershore Road, Cotteridge, Kings Norton and West Heath

Turning out of Pebble Mill Road and crossing Bristol Road is car 803. This air-braked Brush totally enclosed 63hp tram of 1928 was mounted on EMB Burnley bogies. The tram was only transferred to Selly Oak depot in October 1950 when the Washwood Heath services were closed. Car 803 is working on an inbound 36 service from Cotteridge during October 1951. This tram was briefly allocated to Cotteridge depot in 1951 and again during early 1952 when Cotteridge was short of trams. (W.J. Wyse)

Pebble Mill Road was named after the farm on the land between the old turnpike and the confluence between Bourn Brook and the River Rea. It was originally a narrow country lane linking Bristol and Pershore Roads. In 1920 the lane was rebuilt as a dual-carriageway with Birmingham's first central reservation for trams. This became the model for subsequent central reservation schemes in the city's suburbs. Coming down the gentle tree-lined slope of the central reservation in Pebble Mill Road is car 737 a Brush-bodied EMB air-brake bogie car built in 1926 and like all the air-brake cars would be withdrawn when the Bristol Road group of routes were abandoned on 5 July 1952. (M. Rooum)

Just in front of the line of trams parked on the inbound track at the Pershore Road end of Pebble Mill Road is the crossover that was put in place in August 1951. A second crossover was built at the Bristol Road end of the central reservation. This was so that up to twenty trams could be parked while the conversion of both Selly Oak and Cotteridge depots to buses was taking place. The single line working was controlled by traffic signals. Tram 779 is parked at the rear of the line near to the Pershore Road junction on 27 April 1952. (A.N.H. Glover)

After the Pershore Road trams were abandoned, the replacement 45 bus service left the city centre by way of Belgrave Road instead of Pebble Mill Road. 1560 (JOJ 560), a 1947 Daimler CVG6 with an MCCW H30/24R body, has travelled past Calthorpe Park in Pershore Road and is crossing the entrance to Edward Road. This area on the borders of Balsall Heath and Edgbaston marked a blurring in the historical development of Birmingham; behind the bus are the well-built Victorian villas with gabled attics while to the left are some of the equally large interwar semi-detached houses. (J. Whitmore)

During the months after August 1951 when trams were stabled in Pebble Mill Road, a nightwatchman ensured that the trams were not damaged. In May 1952, car 840 has just passed the nightwatchman's hut as it turns right into Pershore Road. This Short-bodied, totally enclosed 63hp air-brake tram mounted on M&T Burnley bogies entered service in April 1929. Beyond the tram are the wide open spaces of the 80-acre Cannon Hill Park, which had originally been donated to the town of Birmingham by Miss Louisa Ryland and opened on 1 September 1873. (D.R. Harvey collection)

On 11 January 1952, bogie car 756 travels into the city along Pershore Road when working on the 36 route. It is following a 1948 Triumph 1800 two-seat Roadster. On the right is the Selly Oak depot of the recently nationalised British Road Services who had taken over the combined yard of both Evans and Brookvale Haulage Companies. The late Victorian terraced housing on this section of Pershore Road had attic windows and distinctive continuous roofs over the ground-floor bay windows. (D.J. Norton)

Passing the small 1850s terrace in Pershore Road near the junction with Kitchener Road are two 1950s and '60s stalwarts of Cotteridge garage. The leading bus is 3034 (MOF 34), a Guy 'Arab' IV with a Metro-Cammell body, which, when new in July 1953, had been involved on the last day changeover from trams to buses on the Erdington routes. 3034 is working on the fairly unusual 41D shortworking to Staple Lodge Road near to Turves Green. Following behind is Daimler CVG6 1560 (GOE 560), which is working back to Cotteridge garage. (A.B. Cross)

Travelling towards Stirchley in Pershore Road on the 36 route, Short-bodied Maley & Taunton bogie air-brake car 816 has just passed the tram pinch road sign which showed motorists that the curve of the road and the curve of the tram tracks were not the same. A distant Midland Red Brush forward entrance SOS FEDD has just passed Selly Park Girls' School and is about to cross the Dogpool Lane junction as it travels out of the city on its way to Alvechurch and Redditch on a 147 service. (F.N. Lloyd Jones)

On its first day in service, 7 July 1952, 2806 (JOJ 806), a Daimler CVG6 with a Crossley H30/25R body, pulls away from the new bus stop outside the Pavilion cinema and passes over the bridge across Griffins Brook near the corner of Cartland Road. These stylishly finished buses were only used briefly on the Pershore Road service which soon became the preserve of the similar-looking Metro-Cammell-bodied Guy 'Arab' IVs. The recently abandoned tramlines and overhead cables were last used

on Sunday 6 July when lightweight tram 842 became the last to leave Cotteridge depot. The Pavilion cinema was opened on 28 November 1931 and in 1960 was the first of three cinemas in Birmingham to be partially converted into a bowling alley. (D. Griffiths)

It is business as usual as passengers board the tram outside the Ten Acres and Stirchley Co-op on a warm day in the spring of 1952. The tram is at the city end of the one way system in Hazelwell Street near to the junction with Umberslade Road and the Three Horseshoes public house. The Short Bros totally enclosed bogie car 832 is working on the usual 36 service and has just been overtaken by a Midland Red S13 single-decker working on the 147 route from Redditch. The bus stop on the left, soon to be used by the replacement Pershore Road buses, was at this time being used solely by the single-deck operated 27 route coming from the Cadbury factory at Bournville. (C. Carter)

The Ten Acres and Stirchley Co-operative Society seemed to dominate the city end of both Pershore Road and Hazelwell Street. Leyland 'Olympic' HR 40 2263 (JOJ 263) loads up at the bus stop outside TASCO's premises in Pershore Road on 29 August 1951. This building had the peculiar combination of a lending library, chemist, coal merchants and optician departments. This underfloor-engined thirty-six-seater is travelling on the 27 route from the nearby Kings Heath towards Bournville. (A.D. Packer)

Open-topped CBT car 162 travels along Pershore Road and is about to pass the Mary Vale Road junction where the knickerbockered boys are standing. Stirchley only really developed after the nearby Birmingham & West Suburban Railway line was opened on 3 April 1876 and attracted further people when the Cadbury Bros chocolate factory began operation in September 1879. The tram is passing through the early 1890s shopping centre on the single track as it heads towards Cotteridge in about 1905. This tram would be taken over by the Corporation in July 1911 and be renumbered as car 507. (D.R. Harvey collection)

In about 1921, after the tram lines had been doubled, car 568 passes along Pershore Road's Stirchley shopping centre. It has just passed the junction with Ivy Road where the van is parked and will shortly reach the original, if briefly used, terminus at Mayfield Road which was used for just five weeks in May and June 1904. This UEC-bodied tram was mounted on M&G Burnley bogies and had still got an open balcony. The shop with the large lantern on the wall was a beer retailer where draught and bottled sales could be purchased for consumption off the premises. (Commercial postcard)

Just before they were replaced by Daimler 'Fleetlines' in 1967, a Metro-Cammell-bodied Guy 'Arab' IV 2943 (JOJ 943) has just crossed the junction with Fordhouse Lane and is about to tackle the steep climb over the Worcester and Birmingham Canal at Breedon Cross. The bus is working on the 41 service to Turves Green. Behind the Morris J2 van on the right is the newsagents shop which was virtually destroyed on 26 October 1942 when Short-bodied bogie car 821 ran away from the Cotteridge terminus and overturned at the end of the 'S' bend over the Breedon canal bridge, demolishing the shop front. On the left is the large Guest, Keen & Nettlefold factory which supplied screws, nuts bolts washers and fastenings to markets all over the UK. (R.F. Mack)

One of Cotteridge depot's ubiquitous 812 class trams, car 838, slowly crests the canal bridge as it begins the long, steep descent to the Fordhouse Lane road junction in late 1951. Just above Breedon Bridge, on the Cotteridge side, is the large Breedon Cross public house on the corner with Lifford Lane. This Victorian pub was a landmark in the area but was closed in 1994, demolished in 2003 and replaced by a new block of flats. On the right is the old Kings Norton Palace of Varieties which opened in 1923 as a silent cinema and music hall. In 1933 it was refurbished and modernised and reopened as the Savoy cinema but was closed on 2 February 1958 and was converted into industrial use, known as Savoy Works. (R.W.A. Jones)

Having climbed the steep hill from the Breedon Cross public house and the nearby canal bridge, Short-bodied bogie car 817 stands at the tram stop at the corner of Frances Road. It is picking up a couple of passengers who are going on the two-stop ride to Cotteridge. Behind the overtaking 1948 Ford Anglia is Cotteridge County Primary School, located on the corner of Breedon Road. This was opened in 1900 by the Kings Norton School's Board as a mixed infants' school with a pupil capacity of 615. (R.B. Parr)

Standing outside the decorated, Gothic-styled St Agnes's church, opened in 1903, is lightweight tram 842. The impressive church was at the northern end of the row of shops in Pershore Road. At the other end was the entrance to Cotteridge terminus. In 1948 this tram still had its low-height English Electric Burnley-style maximum traction bogies with their 26in-diameter driving wheels and before it was re-bogied with the equipment from the former runaway car 821 but after its June 1947 repaint into the post-war livery. This tram, which entered service on 28 November 1929, had a modern good-looking body built by Short Bros and had the distinction of being the only tramcar in the fleet not to have rocker panels. With a capacity of 35/27, car 842 weighed 13 tons 12 cwt 1 qr which was some 3 tons 3 cwt 1 qr lighter than a standard Birmingham bogie tramcar. (D.R. Harvey collection)

Still in the pre-war livery and looking in need of a repaint, car 828 stands opposite the entrance to Cotteridge depot in about 1946. The trolleypole has been turned and the tram driver is waiting for his departure time before leaving on the journey to the city terminus of the 36 route in Navigation Street. Rhodes china shop next to the depot entrance was the last in the impressive Edwardian row of shops in Pershore Road and would remain in Cotteridge until well into the 1980s. (D.R. Harvey collection)

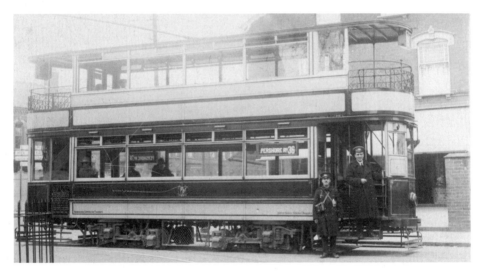

The crew of UEC-bodied car 572 proudly pose on the platform in about 1925. This was not long after these Mountain & Gibson bogie cars arrived at Cotteridge and before the legal lettering was changed from Birmingham Corporation Tramways in 1927. The tram is parked opposite Watford Road, outside the entrance to Cotteridge depot and has still got its open balconies and the wing window opposite the top of the staircase. These trams, including car 572, were replaced in 1928 and 1929 when the entire 812 class were delivered to Cotteridge to work the Pershore Road 36 service. (D.R. Harvey collection)

Car 843, numerically the last Birmingham tram, was the second of the two experimental lightweight tramcars and entered service on 9 September 1930. It was even lighter than its year-older sister car, weighing 12 tons 6 cwt 2 qrs. It is standing opposite the depot and alongside George Mason's grocery shop on the corner of Watford Road in about 1943.

The conductress is turning the trolleypole; if this were at night, she would have the protection of the trough on the overhead which was there to stop any electric arcing being seen from the air. (Burrows Brothers)

Picking up passengers at the bus shelter in Watford Road, Cotteridge, is 1697 (HOV 697), one of Yardley Wood garages Brush-bodied Leyland 'Titan' PD2/1. The bus is working on an 18A service from Northfield to Yardley Wood in 1952, some time after the Bristol and Pershore Road tram abandonments and before the coronation of Queen Elizabeth II. This can be deduced because of the destination display and also because the bus has not been fitted with a coronation flag holder. (C. Carter)

Looking a little dusty, one of the Maley & Taunton air-brake bogie cars, 831, waits at the single-track entrance to Cotteridge depot on 27 June 1952. Standing between the public toilets, this Short Bros-bodied, sixty-two-seat tram, with its eight-windowed top deck is about to take up its duty on the 36 route. In order to reach the inbound track, all trams leaving the depot yard had to turn left to the stub terminus opposite Watford Road and then move over the points to the inbound terminus stop outside George Mason's shop. (G.F. Douglas)

The former tram yard in Cotteridge was converted into a most useful parking area for the replacement buses. The tram depot and yard had a capacity for about thirty-two trams and after conversion there were around thirty-six buses allocated, though up to half of this figure were parked in the yard above the West Birmingham Suburban Railway line. Seven JOJ-registered Guy 'Arab' IVs, with 2929 (JOJ 929) on the left and the easily identified fifty-seven-seat 2926 (JOJ 926) with the Auster front ventilators, stand in Cotteridge yard in 1965. (R.H.G. Simpson)

One of the more usual Corporation buses was 2847 (JOJ 847). This Daimler CVG6 bodied by Crossley, had entered service on 1 November 1952. After turning over in an accident, the bus was rebuilt with platform doors which were fitted at Midland Red's Carlyle Road Works in Edgbaston. The bus re-entered service on 10 December 1959 and spent part of its BCT career allocated to Cotteridge garage. It is working on the 41 service from Turves Green and has just crossed the railway bridge at Kings Norton Station in Pershore Road South. Behind the bus is Cotteridge Fire Station, built in 1930. (L. Mason)

The 47 bus route was first operated on 2 April 1967 and followed the earlier 41 bus route through Turves Green, before crossing Longbridge Lane and terminating in Edenhurst Road near the junction with Grovelly Lane. Dual-doored Park Royal-bodied Daimler 'Fleetline' CRG6LX, 3820 (NOV 820G), entered service in January 1969 and has come down the very steep hill from Cotteridge in Pershore Road South. The bus, owned by West Midlands Travel, is turning into Camp Lane. (D.R. Harvey collection)

Beyond the tram terminus at Cotteridge was Pershore Road South which crossed the deeply incised valley of the river Rea before climbing up to Kings Norton Green. At Kings Norton the suburban 18 and 23 bus services stopped alongside the Junior and Infant School, just short of the Navigation public house on the corner of Wharf Road.

On 6 June 1952, one of the splendid Weymann-bodied Leyland 'Tiger' PS2/1s, 2244 (JOJ 244), picks up passengers at the green-painted bus shelter on its way to West Heath on the soon to be abandoned 23 route. It is being followed by a 1945 West Bromwich-registered Fordson E83A van. Travelling towards Cotteridge on an 18A service is 1664 (HOV 664), another of Yardley Wood garage's Brush-bodied Leyland 'Titan' PD2/1s. (G.F. Douglas, courtesy A.D. Packer)

'The Green' in Kings Norton still retains its earlier 'village' character but lies off the old toll-road and is therefore just off the bus routes. A number of buildings of historic interest surround the Green, in particular St Nicolas church and the Saracen's Head. The church dates back to the thirteenth century and has as its crowning glory a fifteenth-century tower and crocketed spire, which is an impressive landmark visible for several miles. St Nicolas church is larger than the neighbouring Norman church in Northfield and shows us that Kings Norton was the richer parish. The Saracen's Head next door was originally a wool merchant's house but in more recent times has been a public house and a shop. Kings Norton was mainly Royalist during the civil war and Queen Henrietta Maria came to the area leading a replacement army. The Queen slept in the Saracen's Head while the soldiers camped on land behind the church. (D.R. Harvey)

The Old Grammar School stands in the graveyard surrounding the twelfth-century St Nicholas parish church. Dating from the fifteenth century, the Old Grammar School was originally the priest's house and is a two-storey structure with a stone and brick ground floor and a timber-framed upper storey. The school's most famous headmaster was Thomas Hall, a puritanical Protestant who became curate and headmaster of Kings Norton in 1640. After continuing as a school for 200 more years, the building fell into neglect at the beginning of the ninteenth century. Repairs were made in 1910 when a new external staircase was put in. In 2004 it won a BBC2 television restoration prize. (D.R. Harvey)

Standing at the Pool Farm terminus of the 4 route is 2262 (JOJ 262) in Hillmeads Road, one of the five integrally constructed Leyland 'Olympic' HR40s fitted with Weymann B36F bodies. The 4 route to the early 1960s Pool Meadow housing estate was opened on 1 December 1963 and the five thirteen-year-old 'Olympics' were specially converted to one-man operation (OMO), as revealed by the 'pay as you enter' signs. The route ran as a feeder service to connect with the main Pershore Road services and the Outer Circle route in Cotteridge. (L. Mason)

The 41 route was begun on 21 July 1957 to serve the growing Turves Green housing estate. 2926 (JOJ 926) was the modified Metro-Cammell-bodied Guy 'Arab' IV with a two-landing staircase and a seating layout increased to H32/25R. It is working on the 41 route and has crossed West Heath Road from Staple Lodge Road whose multi-storey flats can be seen on the distant skyline. The bus is climbing towards the 1950s Turves Green housing estate in the strangely rural section of the confusingly named Turves Green. (R.F. Mack)

Thirteen months after being introduced, the 41 route was extended from Culmington Road, Turves Green, along Longbridge Lane to a turning circle at Central Drive on 17 August 1957. The route had the advantage of giving another service to the Austin Motor Co.'s Longbridge factory. 2928 (JOJ 928), a 1952 Guy 'Arab' IV with an MCCW H30/25R body, stands in the triangle at the terminus with the distant houses in Tessall Lane just visible beyond the former Midland Railway's Birmingham to Bristol mainline and the valley of the river Rea. Behind the tree would now be the site of Longbridge station on the Cross-City line opened on 8 May 1978. (L. Mason)

The Groveley Lane terminus of the 47 route was hardly half a mile from the Longbridge factory and was actually located in Edenhurst Road. Standing at the terminus alongside the decapitated Bundy Clock and in front of the Jaguar Mark II is 3040 (MOF 40). The Gardner 6LW-engined Guy 'Arab' IV is apparently not doing a lot of business in this suburban housing area located between Turves Green and Longbridge. (L. Mason)

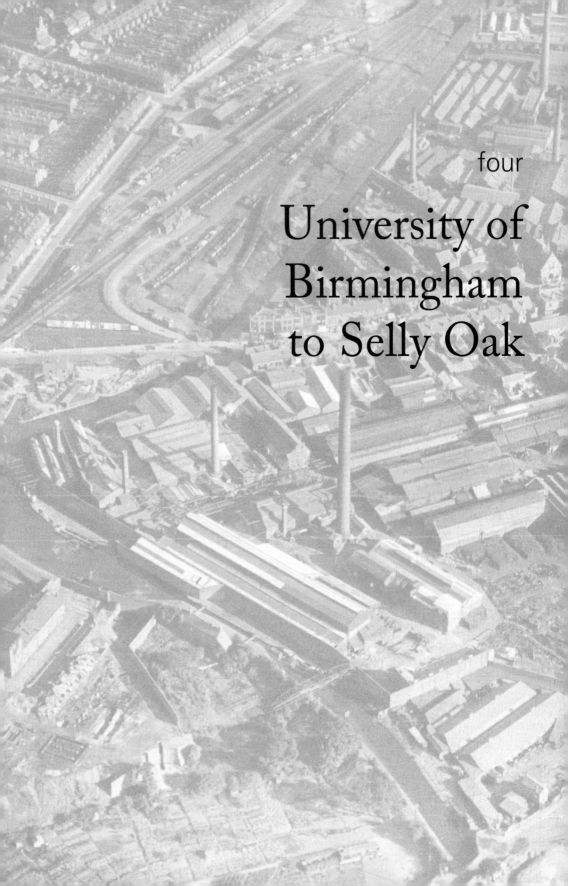

four

University of Birmingham to Selly Oak

BIRMINGHAM UNIVERSITY.

The University of Birmingham was one of the first 'red brick' universities in England, having received its Charter in 1900. Lord Calthorpe offered land at the western Bournbrook end of the Calthorpe Estate and the new buildings were constructed between 1903 and 1909. Although the Byzantine designs of Sir Aston Webb for the new campus were never completed, the first phase of the university was opened on 7 July 1909 by King Edward VII. Joseph Chamberlain was the first Chancellor and Sir Oliver Lodge became the first Principal. These original buildings included the Great Hall and the 325ft-high Tuscan campanile tower known locally as 'Big Joe'. It was designed to resemble the fourteenth-century Torre Del Mangia in Siena. Because of the sloping site, these original buildings stand over Edgbaston and Bournbrook and dominate the suburb. (Commercial postcard)

Thursday 27 July 1950 was a very pleasant sunny summer's day. Car 746, a Brush-bodied air-brake bogie tram, built in 1926, travels towards the city when working on a 72 service from Longbridge. The railings on the far side of Bristol Road guard Bourn Brook which is a tributary of the River Rea and has its confluence within the confines of Cannon Hill Park. Beyond the brook are the late Victorian houses which are not in Bristol Road at all, but in Arley Road, a little dog-leg of a road that runs off Bournbrook Road. (D. Griffiths)

The Brook public house was opened on 16 May 1961 on open land about 50 yards from Dawlish Road. This was the only public house along the Bournbrook and Selly Oak section of Bristol Road to have its own car park. This Mitchells & Butlers house had replaced an old beer house at 536 Bristol Road, but despite being well within the catchment area of the University of Birmingham, the premises were closed and demolished in the early part of the twenty-first century. (Birmingham Central Reference Library)

Looking into the city from the former terminus of the Bournbrook accumulator cars is one of the original CBT 151-171 class, travelling into Birmingham in about 1905. These tramcars had opened the electric overhead tram route on 14 May 1901 when it had been extended to Chapel Lane, Selly Oak. Just out of sight on the left is the Bournbrook Hotel which had opened in 1877. On the far corner of Grange Road is Jackson's furniture store, housed at the end of an impressive row of late Victorian gabled properties. The beer house on the right was replaced by Brook public house in the early 1960s. On the right is Dawlish Road where the CBT tramway depot was located. (Commercial postcard)

The Bournbrook Hotel is a splendid building quite dominating the 'high street' of Bournbrook in Bristol Road. This large, white Victorian building stands on the corner of Bristol Road and Grange Road, which as well as leading to the Ariel Motorcycle factory also gave pedestrian access to the University of Birmingham. The pub was opened by the Holt Brewery to replace the old Malt Shovel Inn in 1877, around the time that Bournbrook was beginning to develop as a suburb. The Mitchells & Butlers-owned Bournbrook Hotel has had a number of name changes in recent years, mainly to encourage the never-ending stream of university students who for a century have used the pub as their local. In recent years it has been called the Flapper & Firkin, Old Varsity Tavern, and today it is called The Goose at the OVT. (D.R. Harvey)

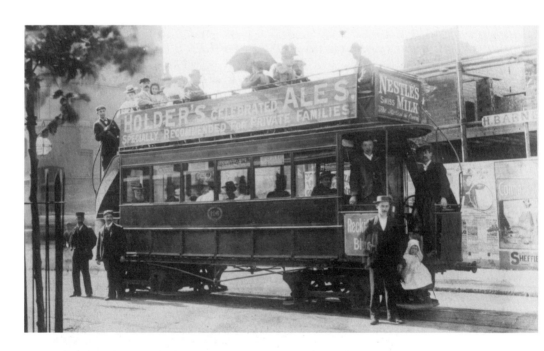

The Birmingham Central Tramways Company (later to become CBT) began operating battery accumulator tramcars from the Suffolk Street junction with Navigation Street to Dawlish Road, Bournbrook, on 24 July 1890. Cars 101–112 were eight-wheel open-top bogie trams built by the Falcon Engine & Car Works of Loughborough. At first glance they looked similar to the contemporary cable cars running on the route to Hockley and Handsworth, although the six panels in the tram's rocker sheet were where the rechargeable traction batteries were housed. Car 106 is parked at the terminus in Bristol Road just short of the turn into the depot located in Dawlish Road. Behind the tram is the still fairly new Bournbrook Hotel as well as some properties that were still under construction. (H.A. Whitcombe collection)

The Bristol Buildings dated from 1887, built at the time of the major expansion of Bournbrook towards Birmingham. Just three years earlier, with the exception of the Bournbrook Hotel and Westley Richards Gun Factory in Grange Road on the banks of Bourn Brook, this area north-east of Selly Oak was open countryside. This section of Bristol Road was unofficially known as Bournbrook High Street and was the local shopping area. On a rainy Tuesday, 4 December 1951, a large 1938-vintage Austin 2½-litre car leaves the Tiverton Road junction with Barclays Bank on the corner and proceeds past some Birmingham-based chain city-wide stores such as Foster Bros, gentlemen's outfitters, the Co-operative butchers shop, whose frontage is being cleaned by the butcher's boy, and finally the Maypole Dairy, who were provisions merchants. There is not a tram in sight! (Birmingham Central Reference Library)

Midland Red used Bristol Road to gain access to Barnt Green, Redditch, Bromsgrove, Worcester and the Malvern area, the last three being served by the long 144 route. In 1951 there were thirty-seven daily journeys between Station Street in Birmingham's City Centre and Malvern Wells, usually with three trips an hour. During the week this was timed at 2 hours 22 minutes. A barely one-year-old 3517 (MHA 517), a BMMO D5 with a Brush H30/26R body, is following a BCT Daimler CVA6 working on the 2B route through Bournbrook as it takes a full load out of Birmingham. (J. Cull)

A batch of fifty Leyland-bodied Leyland 'Titan' PD2/1s were delivered to the Corporation between the end of March and June 1949. Some of them were intended to work on the 2B service between Kings Heath and the Ivy Bush via the Queen Elizabeth Hospital which necessitated running beneath the railway bridge in Dads Lane, Kings Heath. Between the order being placed and the delivery of these buses the roadway under Dads Lane Bridge was lowered. These Leylands, which were about 7in lower than a standard Birmingham bus, were not now needed for the 2B route. 2154 (JOJ 154) entered service on 12 May 1949 and is seen here climbing Bristol Road just before Heeley Road and the railway bridge. Behind it is the Arts & Crafts mock-Tudor-styled Selly Oak Institute, opened in 1894 costing £5,500, donated by George Cadbury. (J. Cull)

The steam from a locomotive passing over Selly Oak bridge billows into the sky as a 301 class tram leaves Selly Oak on its way into Birmingham on a 71 service on 2 February 1937. It is noticeable that there is hardly any vehicular traffic other than the tram. The boy is obviously having problems with the chain on his bike as leans over the machine at the kerb outside one of Harry Payne's shoe repair shops. These smaller shops would have dated from the 1870s while the three-storey premises nearer to the railway bridge were known as the Commercial Buildings and dated from 1903. On the left are the premises of the Battery & Metal Co. (Birmingham Central Reference Library)

Opposite below: The Birmingham West Suburban Railway line, opened by the Midland Railway in 1876, crossed Bristol Road by way of the bridge just to the north of Selly Oak railway station. Along with the bridges at Aston Station and Dudley Port, Selly Oak railway bridge was classified as a low bridge and could only just be squeezed under by trams with a height of 15ft 6in to the top of the trolley plank. The 301 and 401 classes of four-wheelers could get under the bridge, as could all of the totally enclosed bogie cars numbered from tram 512. All carried a brass plate stating that they could pass beneath these three railway bridges. On 7 June 1952, Brush air-brake bogie car 795, working into Birmingham on a 72 service from Longbridge, is about to pass under the bridge, through which can be seen the Great Hall of the University of Birmingham. (J.H. Meredith)

The introduction of the CBT overhead electric tram service on Tuesday 14 May 1901 enabled the company to extend the route south-westwards along Bristol Road by almost another half mile. The new terminus was a few yards short of Chapel Lane at the Plough & Harrow public house in Selly Oak. CBT tramcar 163, one of the original batch of forty-eight-seat cars built by ER&TCW in 1901, waits at the terminus in about 1908, prior to returning to Navigation Street which had been used as the City terminus since 4 February 1902. (Commercial postcard)

An aerial view over Selly Oak in about 1930 shows the whole of the centre of the suburb in wonderful detail. With west at the bottom of the photograph, the ill-fated Dudley No.2 Canal to Blowers Green, Dudley, by way of the troublesome Lapal Tunnel, winds its way under the hump-back bridge in Harborne Lane which was rebuilt during 1930. The canal passes around Elliott's rolling mill, with its two large chimneys, which was established in 1844 and was known for the production of patent sheathing metal for the shipping industry. At the rear of the factory the Dudley No.2 Canal joins with the main-line Worcester & Birmingham Canal, opened in 1795. Running parallel to this canal is the former Midland Railway's Birmingham West Suburban line, opened in 1876. Selly Oak Station and the goods marshalling yards surround the station. Both the railway and the canal pass under Bristol Road, which runs across the view from north to south. To the east are rows of Victorian terraced tunnel-back houses dating from the 1870s and 1880s. At the junction with Chapel Lane, where the steep roof of St John's Church stands opposite the Oak cinema, a BCT bogie car travels into the City and through Selly Oak's shopping centre, followed by two members of the open-balconied 301 class. On the third side of the triangle is Chapel Lane where an AEC 'Regent' bus is working towards Selly Oak tram depot on an 11 bus service. (Birmingham Central Reference Library)

Opposite below: The Plough & Harrow public house on the corner of Chapel Lane was built in the late nineteenth century when it was known as the New Inn; it was renamed in 1904. On the right, on the corner of Elliott Road, is St John's Methodist church which was built in 1876 and greatly enlarged in 1908. In July 1952 car 737, one of the 1926-built Brush totally enclosed, air-brake cars has just crossed the access tracks in the foreground, which led to Selly Oak depot, as it travels into Birmingham on a 71 service. Behind the tram is the Regency-styled early Victorian Dog & Partridge public house that closed in 1997. (J.S. Webb)

On 7 June 1952 one of the 1928 vintage, Brush totally enclosed, EMB air-brake bogie cars, tram 784, travels down Chapel Lane as it returns to Selly Oak depot in company with a Fordson 5 cwt van. These former Washwood Heath-based trams were not popular with Selly Oak drivers because of their complicated air-brake systems. The early Victorian terrace on the right next to the Plough & Harrow Hotel seems strangely out of place next to the huge brick expanse of the Birmingham Battery factory. (R.B. Parr)

The Weoley Castle housing estate was begun in the early 1930s and, following the example set by the earlier Kingstanding housing development, relied on buses rather than trams for public transport. The first Weoley Castle bus service began on 17 October 1932, while the 20X service was one of six new services initiated into the huge municipal development on 24 February 1937. This was a circular route from Selly Oak via Weoley Park Road, Shenley Fields Road and to Castle Square, returning via Gibbins Road and into Harborne Lane. Standing at the Selly Oak terminus in Chapel Lane opposite the Oak cinema on 17 June 1952 is Metro-Cammell-bodied Daimler COG5, 1048 (CVP 148), a bus that dated from 1937 and lasted until 1960. (A.D. Packer)

five

Selly Oak Depot/Garage

Selly Oak depot was opened on 12 July 1927 with a capacity of eighty trams on ten roads, as well as having a capacity for about forty buses. It replaced the former CBT tram depot in Dawlish Road and was built at the bottom of Chapel Lane in Harborne Lane and was also briefly used as the bus body paint works. Beneath the Dutch-style gables and through the large entrance doors is an ADC 507 double-decker 271 (OX 1547), with a locally built Buckingham body. On the left are two 301-class four-wheeled trams. Harborne Lane was still a single-track road through the countryside to Harborne and would not be widened until 1929. (Birmingham Central Reference Library)

Opposite below: Selly Oak was the only one of the Corporation premises built to accommodate both buses and trams. The garage opened on July 1927 and in 1946 was allocated some wartime Guy 'Arab' IIs to augment its pre-war fleet of early Daimler COG5s. 1402 (FOP 402), a Guy 'Arab' II, entered service on 1 March 1945 and was the second of a pair fitted with a rather gaunt-looking Strachan body. The bus stands on the forecourt of the garage in about 1949. It was taken out of service on 30 April 1950. (J. Cull)

In early July 1952, with the abandonment notices in its windows, car 807, a Brush-bodied, EMB air-brake car mounted on EMB Burnley bogies dating from January 1929, stands on the forecourt of Selly Oak depot, while just inside the doors is the earlier tram car 517. Inside the garage are some of the brand new buses that would enter service on Sunday 6 July 1952. Selly Oak had some fifty-five new vehicles, including 2776-2800 from the Crossley-bodied Daimler CVG6s and Guy 'Arab' IVs 2901–2920. (D.R. Harvey collection)

The bus fleet introduced to replace the Bristol and Pershore Road trams in July 1952 remained remarkably stable over the years. 2311 (JOJ 311), a Crossley DD42/6 with a Crossley H30/24R body, dating from New Year's Day 1950, had been drafted in from Acocks Green garage, while MCCW-bodied Guy 'Arab' IV 2912 (JOJ 912) entered service on Sunday 6 July 1952. The Crossley was withdrawn on 31 May 1966, but the Guy lasted until 2 August 1971, well into the WMPTE era. It was normal practice to park buses on the forecourt of the garage. On the other side of Chapel Lane was the imposing high brick wall of the factory end of the Birmingham Battery Co. who made brass and copper tubes. (A.D. Broughall)

The right-hand side of the BCT premises at Selly Oak was used to house buses and was equipped with fuel pumps. Over twenty years separates the dates of the introduction of these two buses standing inside Selly Oak garage in 1971. 2621 (JOJ 621), a 1951 MCCW-bodied Guy 'Arab' III Special, stands alongside the year-old 3938 (SOE 938H), an eighty-seat Daimler 'Fleetline' CRG6LX/33. The Guy would be withdrawn on 31 March 1975, being outlived by the 'Fleetline' by only four and a half years. On the left is 3942 (SOE 942H), another of the 'Jumbos'. Selly Oak garage was finally closed on 2 August 1986. (D.R. Harvey collection)

six

Selly Oak

The Oak cinema, built in Bristol Road on the corner of Chapel Lane, was opened on 26 March 1923. Looking towards Northfield, the construction of the new tracks is taking place for the 35 route extension to Northfield, which opened on 1 October 1923 as the 69 route. In the late summer of 1923 the Oak is showing the 1922 silent film *A Bill of Divorcement*, which was a film adaptation of actress and playwright Clemence Dane's (aka Winifred Ashton, 1888–1965) very successful 1921 London stage play starring Constance Binney and Fay Compton. This play was a strange mixture of melodrama and social problems and was a 'weepie'. The Oak eventually closed on 3 November 1979 with the film *Quadrophenia* and was demolished in December 1984. (Birmingham Central Reference Library)

Opposite below: On 7 June 1952, car 535, one of the former open-balconied UEC-bodied trams of 1913, mounted on Mountain & Gibson Burnley maximum-traction bogies, stands outside Singleton's grocery shop next to the set-back Oak cinema and the distant Chapel Lane. Car 535 was one of twenty-five trams to be fitted with GEC 70hp motors in 1927 which enabled them to operate very quickly on the reserved sections of track along the Bristol Road routes. 535 is only working as far as Pebble Mill Road while in front of it car 558, a 63hp car, is city-bound on a 71 service. (R.B. Parr)

Nearly thirty years later, on 11 June 1952 the scene in Selly Oak had hardly changed. The Oak was showing two 1951 films, Mitzi Gaynor in *The Golden Girl* and Jeannie Crain in *The Model and the Marriage Broker*. The leading tramcar at the Chapel Lane crossover outside the Oak cinema is 623. This all-electric Brush-bodied sixty-two-seater was mounted on Brush Burnley bogies and re-motored with DK30/1L 63hp motors. Destined to become the penultimate tramcar at the final closure, car 623 was one of just nine of the 587 class to have its body strengthened in 1948. It is working into Birmingham on the 69 service from Northfield. The second tram is air-brake car 752 which is also inbound but is working on a 71 service from Rednal. (G.F. Douglas)

Selly Oak was the inner suburban terminus for the first bus services introduced by Birmingham Corporation Tramways. The Birmingham's second new Corporation bus service was begun on 5 November 1913 as a feeder from the Selly Oak tram terminus to the Rose & Crown public house in Rubery. A one-year-old car, 389, a UEC-bodied four-wheel tram stands in Bristol Road at the Chapel Lane terminus and is sandwiched between the Plough & Harrow public house and St John's Methodist church. Standing at the bus shelter is bus 4 (OA 1604), a Daimler 40hp with an LGOC O18/16RO body. All ten of the barely one-year-old Daimler chassis were impressed by the War Department and were presumably lost in the First World War. (D.R. Harvey collection)

Car 329 had been a Witton depot tram for all of its life until it was transferred to Moseley Road depot on 27 November 1948 as one of six one-for-one replacements for already withdrawn air- and oil-brake 401 trams. So, what is the reason for 329's presence on Selly Oak on 17 April 1949 working an inbound 70 service from Rednal? It was a sunny spring Saturday and with nearly all Selly Oak depot's allocation of 100 tramcars out on the road, this tram was drafted in from Moseley Road to work to Rednal which was common practice for Moseley Road to help move the day trippers to the Lickey Hills. (D.R. Harvey collection)

Standing outside Truman's butchers shop and the Selly Oak branch of George Mason's grocery shop at 806 Bristol Road on 12 October 1949 is 2183, (JOJ 183). The bus is a Park Royal-bodied Leyland 'Titan' PD2/1 and is brand spanking new, having entered service just four days earlier. The bus is working on the 2B route from Kings Heath. This service turned into Bristol Road from Dawlish Road where it passed the old CBT tram depot and is approaching Harborne Lane where it will turn right and go by way of the Queen Elizabeth Hospital and Harborne to the Ivy Bush terminus at Hagley Road. (J. Cull)

The Outer Circle 11 service crossed Bristol Road in the middle of Selly Oak. On the anti-clockwise service the 11 service passed Selly Oak garage before climbing Chapel Lane, turning right into Selly Oak's main shopping centre on Bristol Road. The buses then turned left into Oak Tree Lane before heading off towards Bournville. On 21 October 2007, the author's preserved 1950 Crossley DD42/6, 2489 (JOJ 489), stands at the new bus shelter, next to the tree that, incidentally, is not the 'Selly Oak'! 2489 is working on an historic replication of the Outer Circle route. In the half century since the trams departed the Victorian shops on this side of the shopping centre have surprisingly survived, although they have all lost their chimney stacks. (D.R. Harvey)

The Old Oak Tree in Selly Oak grew just inside Oak Tree Lane, yards from the Bristol Road junction. In 1894 the tree was beginning to look a little sorry for itself due to the construction in 1880 of the houses on the right in Oak Tree Lane. These houses slowly deprived the oak tree of its water supply and the tree turned into a hollow stag oak. When felled in May 1909 it was the symbolic moment when Selly Oak changed from a recognisable village into a suburb of Birmingham. Beyond the houses in Oak Tree Lane, on the other side of Bristol Road, is the gable end of the Oak Inn; on the other side of Harborne Lane is a row of much earlier nineteenth-century properties. (Birmingham Central Reference Library)

A freshly repainted Guy 'Arab' IV, 2950 (JOJ 950), with an MCCW H30/25R body 'steams' across the traffic lights at the Oak Tree Lane junction as it leaves the bustling Selly Oak shopping centre in about 1965 when working on a 61 service to Egghill Lane Estate. Following the Corporation bus is Midland Red 5325 (6325 HA), a Carlyle H40/32RD-bodied BMMO D9 which is only fourteen minutes into its 2-hour 22-minute journey on the 144 service to Malvern Wells via Worcester. (Photograph by Fives)

The row of cottages in Bristol Road in the 1894 photograph of the Old Oak Tree was replaced by a petrol filling station. The terrace on the left, behind the tram, was next to St Mary's school. The tram on the 71 route from Rubery is Brush-bodied air-brake car 740 which had entered service on 6 October 1926. In July 1951, 740 is picking up passengers in the middle of the inbound side of the road which was becoming increasingly hazardous for intending passengers with cars passing on the nearside between a loading tram and the pavement. (J. Cull)

St Mary's school was built in the nineteenth century and finally demolished as part of the 1980s Oak Tree Lane/ Harborne Lane road improvement scheme. However, on 4 July 1951, the school was still in use as two trams pass each other at the south-western end of Selly Oak. On the right is a Belisha Beacon, introduced in 1934 as pedestrian crossings, though by 1951 the black and white road markings were made compulsory, becoming zebra crossings. It is doubtful that the road had been painted by this time. Car 806, one of the Brush totally enclosed, EMB bogie, air-brake cars of 1928, is about to unload a passenger when working on the 70 service while car 733 travels to Pebble Mill Road and is being passed by a rare Austin A70 Hampshire saloon car. (J. Cull)

Also travelling into the city centre, but about eleven years later, is one of the many Midland Red buses that traversed Bristol Road on their way out of the city towards Rednal, Bromsgrove and Worcester. An almost new BMMO D9, 4917 (917 KHA), built in 1961, is passing St Mary's school, Selly Oak, when working on the 144 service from Worcester. These seventy-two-seater 'homemade' Midland Red buses were powerful, mechanically advanced and with their short wheelbase and set-back front axle, were highly manoeuvrable and a joy to drive. (R.H.G. Simpson)

Many of the trams that pulled up to the wartime shelter in Bristol Road at Selly Oak only six days earlier were by 11 July 1952 standing, awaiting their fate, on the reserved tracks in Edgbaston. Although the tram tracks and overhead are still in place, the people waiting at the new stops are now looking for a bus instead. Behind the lovely July 1936-registered Riley 1½-litre Kestrel saloon are the late 1920s premises with flatted accommodation above the shops. These shops were built at a different alignment to the as the intension was to widen Bristol Road between Oak Tree Lane and Langleys Road where the large semi-detached Victorian villa is located. (Birmingham Central Reference Library)

The new reserved tram track towards Northfield was opened on 1 October 1923 when the 69 service was inaugurated. Looking out of the city towards Weoley Park Road, this section of Bristol Road was still largely a rural landscape between Selly Oak and Northfield. As per normal in urban geography theory, once the tramway infrastructure had been opened the urban development and infilling soon followed although in 1924 the lack of housing suggested that the extension to Northfield was something of a speculative venture by the Tramways Department. (Birmingham Central Reference Library)

The railway had reached the village of Selly Oak in 1876 and this was the catalyst for both a rapid industrial and residential growth that had been largely completed before the end of the century. The exception was St Mary's church which was consecrated in September 1861 when Selly Oak was still part of Northfield Parish. This church consisted of a chancel, a nave, transepts and a tower with an attractive spire and was located between Lodge Hill Road and Weoley Park Road. It was designed by E. Holmes in a very basic Victorian Decorated-Gothic style in two colours of sandstone that gave a pleasantly stripy exterior and interior. (Birmingham Central Reference Library)

Car 781, another of the former Washwood Heath bow-collector cars that had been transferred to Selly Oak depot, leaves Selly Oak and joins the reserved track beyond Langleys Road on 1 May 1952 when working on the 71 to Rubery. The late 1920s mock-Tudor, semi-detached houses were only built as far as the top of Griffin Hill before the grounds of Fircroft College was reached. Behind the tramcar is a GOE-registered Daimler CVG6 which is carrying a radiator-mounted destination slipboard for one of the many variations on the Weoley Castle Estate bus service maze! (R.B. Parr)

On 15 May 1965, one of Selly Oak garage's original tram replacement buses, 2906 (JOJ 906), travels out of Selly Oak on the 63 service to Rubery and is approaching the junction with Weoley Castle Road. In the background are the large interwar houses. This bus was a Guy 'Arab' IV with a Gardner 6LW 8.4-litre engine and a Metro-Cammell H30/25R body and was one of thirty buses released for service on 1 July 1952. Following behind is one of the 1950 Guy 'Arab' III Specials, 2527 (JOJ 527), which is operating on the 62 route to Rednal. (Photograph by Fives)

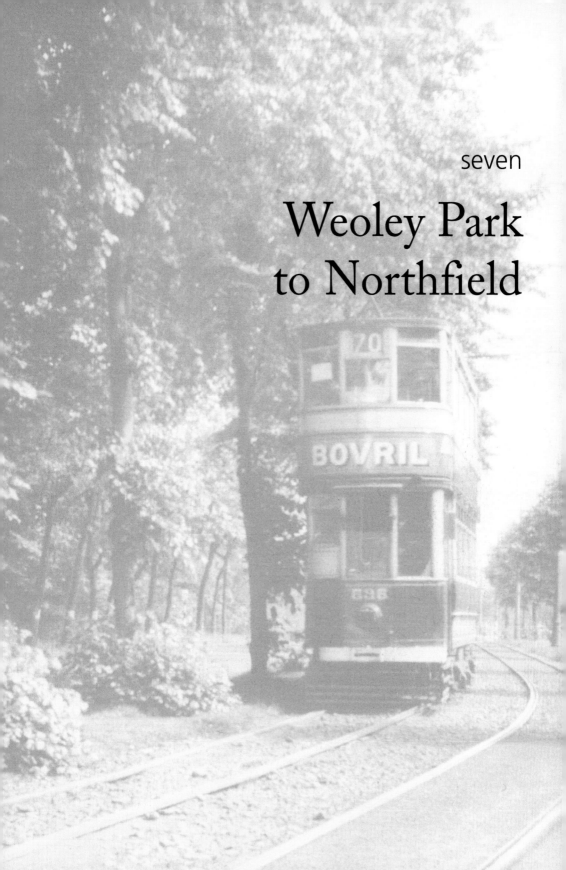

seven

Weoley Park
to Northfield

Having been re-motored with GEC WT 70hp motors in 1927 and fitted with totally enclosed balconies, the first twenty-five UEC-bodied 512 class tramcars of 1913 were the most powerful in the fleet and were noted for their high-speed running on the reserved tracks on the routes to Rednal and Rubery. In 1951, one of these trams, 533, travels inbound when working on a 71 service from Rubery. It has crossed the gap at Weoley Park Road, having climbed the steep Griffin's Hill. On the right is a former military wartime Standard 12hp utility van. (J.S. Webb)

On a sunny day with the tram driver having pulled the canvas sunblind down, open-balconied four-wheel car 379 begins the descent of Griffin's Hill. The tram is working on the 71 service to Rubery in about 1932. On the right are the wooden fences which guarded the Arts & Crafts-styled Fircroft House of 1902 which at this time was still the home of George Cadbury Junior. This architectural style was also found in the original part of the nearby Cadbury-built garden village at Bournville. The Fircroft House was converted into part of the Selly Oak teacher training complex in 1957 and survives today. (Travel Lens Photographic)

When working inbound on a 70 service, car 748 has just passing Witherford Way. On a sunny day in 1951, this 63hp Brush-bodied air-brake tramcar is about to power its way up Griffins Hill towards Selly Oak. Most noticeable is the amount of trees and hedges that lined this part of Bristol Road. The lack of urban development in the 2 miles between Selly Oak and Northfield was largely due to the land being owned by either the Methodist church or the Cadbury-owned Bournville Village Trust. (D.R. Harvey collection)

In June 1931, four-wheeled, UEC-bodied open balcony tramcar 389 has just passed the junction with Middle Park Road. On the left, beyond the motorcycle combination is the Witherford Motor garage whose petrol pumps are alongside the road. The tram is working on an inbound 69 service from Northfield and will shortly pass Witherford Way and begin the climb up Griffin's Hill towards Selly Oak. On the right travelling towards Northfield is a Ford Model T with a van body which positively dwarfs the chassis! (Birmingham Central Reference Library)

At the point where Bournville Lane and Middle Park Road cross Bristol Road, the main A38 road becomes Bristol Road South. In about 1942, car 557, one of the re-motored 63hp UEC-bodied bogie cars of 1913, equipped with wartime headlight masks and white-painted fenders, travels towards Bournville Lane from Northfield on a 72 working to Longbridge. The bridge parapets of the tiny Griffins Brook are visible on both sides of the road. On the right going towards Northfield is a Ford 7W Ten saloon of about 1938. The street furniture signs would really excite a modern-day collector. (Birmingham Central Reference Library)

From the 1952 bus takeover until 1967 Selly Oak had an allocation of exposed radiator Crossleys. 2316 (JOJ 316), a Crossley DD42/6 with a Crossley H30./24R body, had the earlier and less efficient cross-flow Crossley HOE7/4B engine, but did have the lower ratio back axle. This meant that it had a reasonable turn of speed and could maintain the fast-running schedules necessary on the dual carriageway sections of Bristol Road. As a Hillman Minx Series V travels along the far side of the dual-carriageway into the city, 2316 speeds towards the end of the old tramway reserved track near to the junction with Cob Lane in about 1965 when working on the 62 route to Rednal. (R.H.G. Simpson)

One of the splendid Daimler DC27 ambulances belonging to City of Birmingham Ambulance Service disappears down Griffins Brook Lane in June 1951. Car 801, one of the Brush-bodied EMB air-brake eight-wheelers, built in 1928, travels over the gap in the central reservation as it travels toward Northfield on a 71 service to Rubery. The tram has on its balcony panel one of the iconic Birmingham tram advertisements of the early 1950s for St Martins Chunky Marmalade. (D.R. Harvey collection)

An early post-war Jaguar 2½-litre saloon travelling towards Birmingham has overtaken Brush totally enclosed car 804. The tram is about to take the turn at the bottom of White Hill, Bristol Road South, when working on a 71 service in June. Near to the Midland Red bus stop is the entrance to Northfield Manor House. This mock-Tudor Victorian house had been completed in 1864 and had been lived in by George Cadbury from 1894 until the death of his wife Elizabeth in 1951. It is now part of the University of Birmingham campus. Although a working farm, Manor Farm was reconstructed in the 1890s with a large barn where on summer weekends teas, cakes and refreshments were provided for parties of Bournville employees and their families which continued until 1939. (A.W.V. Mace)

Still in its pre-war livery, 70hp, sixty-two-seat car 535 takes the curve in Bristol Road's reserved track at Hole Lane during the wartime summer of 1944. The tram is travelling towards Selly Oak from Northfield and is working on a 70 service from Rednal. The reserved track along Bristol Road was built on concrete sleepers and provided a very smooth ride for most of its life though during the final months, with a lack of maintenance, trams were not allowed to pass each other at speed as a minor accident had occurred when two passing trams touched each other at speed. Empty trams speeding back to Selly Oak depot had been recorded as reaching well over 45mph, but this event stopped this happening permanently. (D. Caton)

Accidents do happen! In about 1959, a collision occurred between Metro-Cammell-bodied Guy 'Arab' III Special 2603 (JOJ 603) and a Morris Oxford Mk III in Bristol Road South, Northfield, on White Hill between White Hill Lane and the Woodlands Hospital. With the former tramway central reservation disappearing into the background – as the A38's dual carriageway – the accident left the Morris Oxford shunted into a lamp post and the back end of the car considerably shortened by the impact. The bus, working on the 62 bus route to Rednal, had a badly damaged nearside front wing and a bent front axle. Ouch! (L. Mason)

In 1951, car 758 passes the entrance to the Woodlands Hospital. This Brush-bodied, totally enclosed, air-brake tram is working towards Northfield, despite the front destination box showing 'DEPOT ONLY'. This 1926-built tram spent all of its life working from Selly Oak depot, although for the first year of its life it was one of the last six of the 732 class to operate from the original former CBT depot in Bournbrook. The Woodlands was a large house, remodelled in 1840, bought by chocolate manufacturer and Quaker philanthropist George Cadbury in 1909. The Woodlands was donated by him as a convalescent home for the Birmingham Crippled Children's Union and today is the Royal Orthopaedic Hospital. (S.L. Eades)

The Travellers Rest public house replaced a Victorian hostelry which was basically a single-storey building with three ground floor bay windows. It was designed by the architectural firm of Bateman & Bateman who specialised in brewery commissions and was built in Cotswold limestone with leaded windows and a thatched roof. The Traveller's Rest was built on the corner of Bristol Road South and Bell Lane and opened on 21 May 1926 next to a row of five very early Victorian cottages. On 14 July 1941 the thatched roof was destroyed by fire, while the pub itself was demolished in 2005 to make way for the new Northfield by-pass which opened two years later. (Birmingham Central Reference Library)

eight

Bournville, Shenley

27 D FRANKLEY BEECHES ROAD BRISTOL ROAD SOUTH

JOJ 246

PAY AS YOU ENTER

The spiritual home of the Leyland 'Tiger' PS2/1s was the 27 service which, after the closure of the Bristol Road tram services, operated on this long inter-suburban service between Kings Heath and West Heath. Both the 10ft-high tunnel beneath the Worcester & Birmingham Canal (and the Birmingham West Suburban Railway line next to it at Bournville station) and the 12ft 6in-high bridge at Northfield Station necessitated the use of single-deckers. In the rush periods, when the Cadbury shift workers came out, the Leylands were loaded to the gunwales. 2246 (JOJ 46) loads up opposite the original red-brick Cadbury factory buildings in 1967 in company with a Marshall-bodied Daimler 'Fleetline' single-decker. (L. Mason)

Standing in Woodlands Park Road at the Hay Green terminus of the 27 route is a pre-war Corporation single-decker. The 27 route had been introduced on 2 October 1935 from Kings Heath to the edge of Northfield by way of Cadbury's Bournville factory. The route was extended on 6 July 1952 when the 23A route was abandoned and the West Heath via Northfield village end of it was subsumed into the extended 27 service. On 1 July 1950, Daimler COG5, fitted with an MCCW B34F body, 55 (AOP 55), looked in good condition despite being withdrawn on the last day of August 1950. The bus had entered service on 7 June 1935, but had spent five years from June 1940 until September 1945 as an emergency ambulance. (A.D. Packer)

2246 (JOJ 246) was one of the fourteen of the class of thirty Weymann-bodied Leyland 'Tiger' PS2/1s to be converted quite late in life to one-man operation in November 1966. These buses were powered by the large Leyland 0.600 9.8-litre engine and as a result had a sparkling turn of speed. They were only 27ft 6in long despite a late abortive attempt to be altered by Weymann to 30ft long prior to delivery. This would have increased the seating capacity from thirty-four to about a more useful thirty-eight seats. The OMO conversion involved a partial removal of the front bulkhead and the insertion of a diagonal window over the rear of the engine bonnet to accommodate the ticket machine. It is near the Dame Elizabeth school in Woodbrooke Road near the Bournville Lido when working on the 27 service towards West Heath. (A.D. Broughall)

The six 36ft-long AEC 'Swift 2P2Rs' had Metro-Cammell B37D bodywork, with spaces for another thirty-nine standing passengers allocated to Selly Oak after a brief sojourn at Acocks Green garage when new. 3680 (KOX 680F), new on 1 October 1967, waits at the Bundy Clock in Woodlands Park Road in 1969 when working on the 27 route. Behind the single-decker is the row of shops in Heath Road behind the bus. (L. Mason)

This Bedford VAM5, FXE 892C, with a rather flimsy Strachan Pacesaver II B46F body, was one of the demonstrators tried out on the newly introduced 20 service. This route was opened on 9 May 1965 and ran from the Bell Lane at Northfield along Shenley Lane as far as Gregory Avenue which was one of the main roads into the 1930s Weoley Castle Estate. The Bedford is waiting in the throat of Gregory Avenue with the Weoley Castle public house to the front of the bus. This lightweight chassis was demonstrated to BCT from 25 November 1965 to 26 February 1966, when it was set against larger rear-engined demonstrators. FXE 892C had a forward-mounted Bedford Diesel engine, a five-speed synchromesh gearbox and three steps into the saloon. FXE 892C was tried out because it was a lightweight vehicle and somewhat perversely led to the ordering of twelve Ford R192s albeit with Strachan bodywork. (A.D. Broughall)

The 20 route was extended further along Shenley Lane from Gregory Avenue as far as Weoley Castle Road on 3 April 1966. It is at this second terminus that the lightweight 3657 (JOL 657E), a Ford R192 with a Strachan B46F body is standing. The Fords were bought to operate on the Express service 99 but were also used when required on the 20 and 27 services, especially out of the peak periods when a double-decker could not be justified. On the opposite side of Shenley Lane are the 1930s detached properties while beyond the oak tree growing in the middle of the central reservation is Barnes Hill. (L. Mason)

The 20 route was extended again on 3 September 1967 via Somerford Road into Weoley Castle's Castle Square. It then left via Castle Road and Alwold Road to Barnes Hill. So the 20 route was back in Weoley Castle for the first time since the original 20 group of routes were renumbered 22 on 21 July 1957, albeit in a different guise running this time from Northfield instead of Selly Oak. 3815 (NOV 815G), a Daimler 'Fleetline' CRG6LX with a Park Royal H43/29D body shows people getting off the bus through the centre exit doors in Somerford Road in about 1968. (L. Mason)

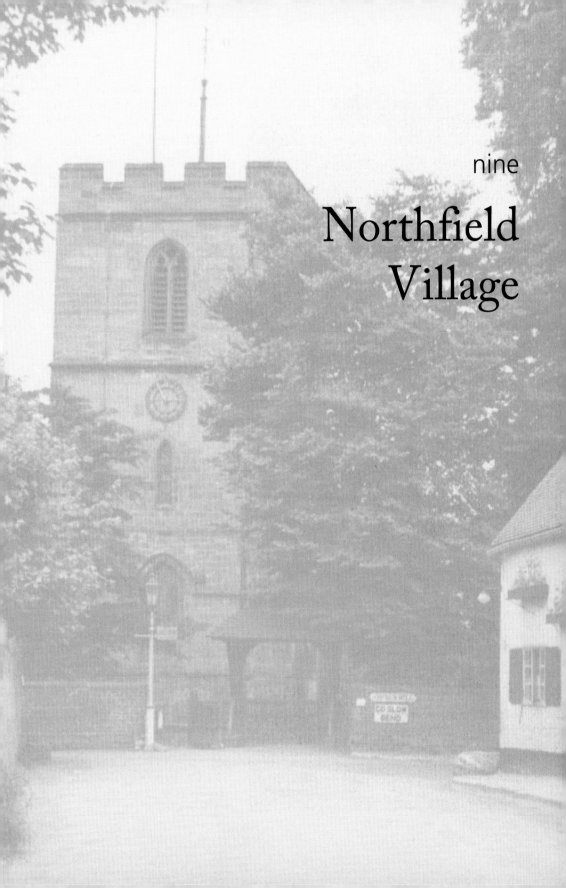

nine

Northfield Village

The village centre of Northfield is around half a mile to the west of the main Bristol Road toll-road and the linear settlement that had eclipsed the size of the original village by 1840. Towards the end of the nineteenth century the old settlement still retains the elements of a pre-industrial village in a rural setting. At the top of the hill is the tower of St Laurence's church and on the eastern side of Church Hill are two distinct rows of eighteenth- and nineteenth-century cottages. At the bottom of the hill is a detached Victorian house dating from the coming of the railway in 1870. Northfield station was the last to be opened on the Midland Railway line in the Birmingham area; the station was enlarged in 1892 when the wooden hut with the corrugated iron roof at the bottom of Station Lane was built. (Birmingham Central Reference Library)

Originally in Worcestershire, from 1889 Kings Norton and Northfield were joined together as an independent Urban District Council. After 1911 both parishes were absorbed into the city as part of the Greater Birmingham Act. The late eighteenth-century Great Stone Inn, based on a much earlier half-timbered building, stands at the top of Church Hill nestling next to the mainly fourteenth-century St Laurence's parish church which was described by Nikolaus Pevsner as having some of the finest Early English work in the county. The Great Stone, a glacial erratic rock, is on the corner of the narrow entrance to Church Hill while to the right of the pub is the sandstone-walled village animal pound. (Birmingham Central Reference Library)

Car 800, a Brush, totally enclosed, air-brake tram of 1928, stands at the Bundy Clock in Northfield. It is outside the early twentieth-century premises of Daniel & Son who sold wallpaper and paint, and Charles Wheeler who, despite the advertisements on his windows for Turf and Woodbine cigarettes and Cadbury chocolate, was a grocer. Car 800, later to become the tram to close the Cotteridge route, is working on a 70 service from Rednal on 7 June 1952. The tram behind is a UEC-bodied bogie cars of 1913; unusually for a Birmingham tramcar, it has a bowed waistrail and a drooping platform. (R.B. Parr)

Birmingham was like many cities where people gave directions by distinctive buildings rather than roads and frequently these key points were public houses. In Northfield there were three hostelries: the Traveller's Rest, demolished in 2005, the Bell Hotel on the corner of Bell Lane, and at the southern end of Northfield the Black Horse. Behind the Austin A70 Hereford is the Bell Hotel, dating from the 1890s, which was demolished in 1983. In front of the A70 is a Morris Eight Series II which is following tramcar 558. This strengthened UEC-bodied bogie car is working on a 70 service from Rednal in 1952. (R.F. Mack)

On Wednesday 1 March 1916, the Rednal bus service was given the route number 5, the Rubery service was numbered 6, the shortworking from Selly Oak to Northfield was the 7 and the Longbridge route which terminated at the Austin factory was the 8. On the right, travelling to Rednal, is a former Midland Red Tilling-Stevens TTA2, 23 (O 9923), built in 1912. It has come from Selly Oak and unloads its passengers at the Bristol Road stop at the corner of Church Lane. The row of shops on the left date from the 1890s and standing outside them is another TTA2. This bus is working in to Selly Oak on the 6 service and is alongside the impressive wooden bus shelter near the corner of Bell Lane, which was only used until the 69 tram route to Northfield was opened on 1 October 1923. (Birmingham Central Reference Library)

In the thirteen months before the First World War, the Corporation bus service from the Selly Oak tram terminus to Rednal and later to Rubery was operated by the ten Daimler petrol-engined 40hp double-decker buses, numbered 1–10. Daimler 7 (OA 1607), working to Rednal, is travelling through Northfield near Rochester Road on an otherwise deserted Bristol Road and has just passed Robert Gillman's garage which a few years earlier had been trading as a cycle shop. In the far distance is the tower of the Bell Hotel. (D.R. Harvey collection)

Sunday 4 May 1952 and the roads look suitably deserted in a time when shops were closed for a day. A rather unkempt-looking 518 unloads a few passengers at the Lockwood Road stop in the middle of Northfield's shopping centre when working the 70 route to Rednal. Car 518 was one of the twenty-five of the 512 class to be re-motored, 70hp motors enabling these UEC-bodied bogie trams to achieve high speeds on the reserved tracks on the Bristol Road routes. By the late 1940s the bodies were rebuilt due to twenty years of strain caused by speeding along Bristol Road. (R.J.S. Wiseman)

Church Road, Northfield, linked the old village of Northfield with the former toll road from Bromsgrove and Worcester which later became the A38 Bristol Road. Loading up in Church Road within sight of the junction with the Bell Hotel is 3666 (KOX 666F), one of the dozen short 33ft-long AEC 'Swift' MPRs with MCW dual-door standee thirty-seven-seater bodies. Generally seen as a poor design, as were most of the mid-1960s generation of rear-engined single-deckers, these AEC 'Swifts' were not really suited to the genteel and meandering 27 route, save for rush hours at the Cadbury Bournville factory. (A. Richardson)

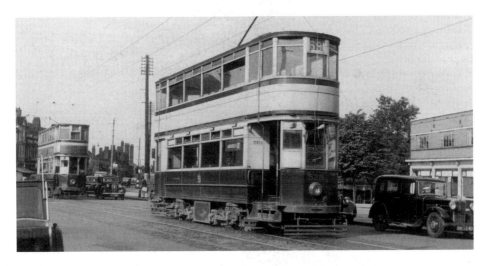

Car 528, a strengthened 70hp car of 1913, stands opposite the Bell Hotel in Northfield with the junction with Church Road on the right. Alongside the tram is a rare Carlisle-registered Morris Ten-Six saloon car dating from 1935. Church Road originally led directly to the old village centre of Northfield around the twin delights of the medieval St Laurence's church and the early eighteenth-century Great Stone Inn. Both Northfield and Selly Oak were notorious bottlenecks along the dual-carriageways of Bristol Road and Bristol Road South, which even in the 1950s was blamed on the trams. Car 528 has arrived at its terminus at the city end of Northfield's busy shopping centre on the 69 route on 28 June 1952 and is being followed by air-brake car 773. (G.F. Douglas)

The inter-urban 18 route between Yardley Wood, Kings Norton, Cotteridge and Northfield was introduced on 20 March 1929. It used Church Road to gain access to Northfield at the Bell Hotel where it turned left into Bristol Road South though the shopping centre before turning right into Frankley Beeches Road at the Black Horse public house. After a number of extensions the 18 service reached the Ley Hill Estate on 6 November 1967. In about 1965, 1524 (GOE 524), a Daimler CVA6 with a Metro-Cammell H30/24R body, running on the 18A service, is being overtaken by a 1948-vintage Brush-body Leyland 'Titan' PD2/1 1691 (HOV 691), operating on a shortworking only as far as the Black Horse pub on the corner of Frankley Beeches Road. (P. Tizard)

The utilitarian yellow-painted litter bins were a feature of Birmingham from the 1960s. 2952 (JOJ 952), a 1952 Guy 'Arab' IV 6LW with an MCCW H30/25R body, passes one of these bins in Northfield's shopping centre in Bristol Road South as it is being overtaken by an Austin Minivan. It is working on the 61 route on 15 May 1965 and is beginning to manoeuvre into the outside lane in order to turn right into Frankley Beeches Road. In the distance near to Lockwood Road is a BMMO C5 coach turning into Digbeth Coach Station on the Birmingham–Worcester motorway express service. (Photograph by Fives)

ten

Allen's Cross, Egghill Lane Estate and West Heath

Before the conversion of the Bristol Road tram routes the 23 single-decker bus service operated between West Heath and Northfield. The Northfield terminus was in Borrowdale Road which gave the Allen's Cross Estate a feeder bus route. 2249 (JOJ 249), one of the 1950-vintage Leyland 'Tiger' PS2/1s with Weymann B34F bodywork, stands at the triangular island in Frankley Beeches Road facing the Black Horse public house on 10 June 1952. Behind the bus is Northfield Methodist church. (G.F. Douglas)

On 10 June 1952, 2249 (JOJ 249), a 1950-vintage Leyland 'Tiger' PS2/1 with a Weymann B34F body, turns out of Hoggs Lane into Frankley Beeches Road after leaving Borrowdale Road terminus. It is heading back towards Bristol Road South in Northfield on a 23 service. To the right of the bus is one of the large 1920s houses which lined Frankley Beeches Road making an interesting comparison to the municipal style housing behind the pedestrians to the left. (A.D. Packer)

The little boy has stopped on his 'fairy cycle' in St Heliers Road, Northfield, to look at the oncoming Guy 'Conquest' C. This Guy B26F-bodied bus 75 (OF 6085) travels along the council house-lined road on the Tinker's Farm Estate. This housing estate and the neighbouring Allen's Cross Estates in Northfield had been farmland until the late 1920s. The bus is working on the 23 service which had been introduced on 30 July 1930. The normal control bus was converted to forward control by Guy Motors at the end of 1931, which neatly dates this scene. (B. Geens collection)

Opposite, below: In Hogg's Lane, Allen's Cross, 3858 (NOV 858G) loads up with passengers at the new 61 route terminus in 1969. Opposite the bus are the serried rows of the early 1930s semi-detached council-built houses in Tudbury Road and in the distance are a later generation of council-built multi-storey flats at the top of Ley Hill which were demolished in 2005. This two-doored, Park Royal-bodied Daimler 'Fleetline' CRG6LX had entered service in March 1969 and only had six months of service with BCT before being taken over by West Midlands PTE. (L. Mason)

Travelling away from Bristol Road South on 6 September 1969 towards the Egghill Lane terminus
in Frankley Beeches Road is 3866 (NOV 866G). This Daimler 'Fleetline' CRG6LX had a Park
Royal H43/289D body and these hundred buses were the first double-doored double-deckers
in the BCT fleet. They had their centre doors fitted with a position on the gearbox after a fatal
accident outside the Traveller's Rest, Northfield, when an elderly lady was caught in the exit doors
and was dragged to her death. (J. Carroll)

The use of single-deckers on the 'main road' routes operated by Selly Oak garage was not common but it did happen if there was nothing else to use. Waiting at the Bundy Clock in about 1962 at the Allen's Cross Estate terminus in Borrowdale Road is 2234 (JOJ 234), a 1950 Weymann B34F-bodied Leyland 'Tiger' PS2/1. It is working on a 61J service but it is showing the archetypally vague SERVICE EXTRA destination. Behind it is 2913 (JOJ 913), one of the Metro-Cammell-bodied fifty-five-seat Guy 'Arab' IVs, which has entered service on 1 July 1952. In 2007 the bus stop was still located at the same spot! Allen's Cross Estate had red-brick cottage-style terraces and a typical 1920s curvaceous road layout with wide crescents and grass verges. The 62 route was extended along Tessall Lane on 15 December 1963. (L. Mason)

The area around Frankley Beeches Road, Tinkers Farm, Egghill Lane, Allen's Farm and Frankley lay undeveloped until after the First World War. As late as 1944 Egghill Lane, looking towards the Birmingham-Worcester boundary, was still rural, though the fence and the pavement on the left was the first sign of the impending construction of the advancing municipal housing estates. In the early 1930s Allen's Cross Estate eventually had 2,161 houses. The new 61 bus route turned into Egghill Lane from Frankley Beeches Road before reaching Norrington Road, so never used this part of this section of the road. (Birmingham Central Reference Library)

The 27 service left Northfield along Bristol Road South when going to West Heath and then turned into South Road. Here, two single-deckers are turning out of South Road and making the awkward manoeuvre across the dual carriageway of Bristol Road South as they turn right and travel up Pigeon House Hill towards Northfield. Halfway across the A38 is 3459 (BON 459C), a 1965 Daimler 'Fleetline' CRG6LX with an unusually styled Marshall B37F body. Following behind is 2255 (JOJ 255), a thirty-four-seat Weymann-bodied Leyland 'Tiger' PS2/1, which would later be preserved. Beyond the 'Fleetline' is Allen's Cross Recreation Ground. (L. Mason)

Emerging from beneath Northfield station's railway bridge is 2237 (JOJ 237). This Leyland 'Tiger' PS2/1 is working towards West Heath on the 27 service in about 1955. Behind the bus is another single-decker from the same class which is beginning the climb to a point halfway up Church Hill, where it turned left into Pamela Road. Northfield railway station was opened by the Midland Railway on 1 September 1870 and survives today as the penultimate station on the electrified Cross-City Line between Longbridge and Lichfield. (B. Geens)

Crossing over the little humpback bridge over the river Rea in West Heath Road, Northfield, is 2265 (JOJ 265), the last of the five Leyland 'Olympic' HR40s. These underfloor-engined, integrally constructed single-deckers were originally going to be the last of the 'Tiger' PS2/1s and the order was amended before construction began. As a result they were the fourth to eighth Olympics to be constructed. They had entered service between the end of July and the beginning of September 1950. The bus has just left the Station Road junction as it heads towards West Heath when working on the 27 route. (L. Mason)

Delivered to Birmingham in April 1967, the twelve lightweight Ford R192s with Strachan B46F bodies were intended to work on the 99 Express Service to Rubery. They were found to be more than useful on other single-deck-operated bus services. Thus, when still quite new, 3658 (JOL 658E) picks up passengers at the Alvechurch Road, West Heath terminus of the 27 route next to the Bundy Clock. The bus is being operated as an OMO vehicle and the driver can be seen issuing bus tickets. In the background, looming over the bus, is the tower of St John Fisher Roman Catholic church. (S.N.J. White)

Eleven

Northfield to Longbridge

In 1965, Guy 'Arab' IV 2912 (JOJ 912) pulls away from the bus stop at the Art Deco-styled Northfield Baths at the south-western end of Northfield's shopping centre when carrying a full load on the 63 service to Rubery. Behind it is another one of the same Metro-Cammell-bodied batch 2949 (JOJ 949) which is working on the 62 service to Rednal. On the left is the amazing Black Horse public house located on the corner of Frankley Beeches Road. Although the public house and the baths remain, the new Northfield by-pass, so needed in tram days, now emerges at a point roughly between the two buses on the opposite side of the road. (Photograph by Fives)

The Black Horse pub is one of the great architectural follies in Birmingham. The original Black Horse Inn was replaced in the late nineteenth century by a double-bay windowed, partially mock-half timbered large public house, attractive enough but like many others in the expanding outer Victorian suburbs. Its replacement was begun in 1924, but the public house was not opened until 1929. It was designed for Davenport's Brewery by Francis Goldsbrough in a mock-Tudor style which hardly misses a sixteenth-century styling trick. It has several large gable ends and is half-timbered throughout on a Cotswold limestone base with a long gallery, a staircase wing and huge casement windows. On 21 July 1971, 'Jumbo' Daimler 'Fleetline' CRG6LX 3955 (SOE 955H) passes the Black Horse when working on a 62 service from Rednal having just left the dual carriageway section at Great Stone Road. (E. Trigg)

Midland Red's 143 service was the Worcester route shortworking. This went as far as Bromsgrove and travelled along the A38. On reaching Longbridge it followed the 70 tram service to Rednal. The journey time to the tram terminus was just 28 minutes with a half-hourly headway and after a 'slog' over the Lickeys it reached the town of Bromsgrove 17 minutes later. A 1954-built BMMO D7, 4109 (THA 109), fitted with a Metro-Cammell H32/26R body speeds passed the Black Horse in Northfield in 1965. (R.H.G. Simpson)

When the Black Horse was opened by Miss Margaret Bondfield, who was Minister for Labour, she seemed to have been totally fooled by the architects as she wrote in the visitors' book, 'This is one of the most beautiful houses I have ever seen.' A man wearing a trilby hat stands in the shade of the young tree in late June 1952 as car 529, with the abandonment notice already in the balcony window, loads up in Bristol Road South before heading off down Pigeon House Hill towards Longbridge and Rednal on a 70 service. Behind the solitary tree is the Northfield Methodist church. (D.R. Harvey collection)

Car 520, one of the UEC bogie trams built in 1913, powers up Pigeon House Hill, Bristol Road South towards Northfield, on a 70 service in 1951. It is about to pass the entrance to South Road on the right. By now transformed into a totally enclosed 70hp tram, these trams could easily travel as quickly as a contemporary private car on the excellent reserved track. By this date, with the abandonment due, the state of the track-bed had deteriorated citing their poor quality in the foreground. (K.G. Harvie)

Travelling along Bristol Road South towards Longbridge is a four-wheel tram working on a 71 service. Car 333 is a UEC top-covered, open-balconied tram mounted on UEC 7ft 6in swing-yoke trucks. It entered service in 1911, and arrived at Bournbrook depot in early 1924 in preparation for the tram extension to Rednal on 14 April 1924. Cat 333 is approaching Hawkesley Mill Lane in September 1937 while on the left is the row of shops near West Park Road. Parked outside these shops is a large, COV-registered Austin 14/6, six-cylindered Goodwood saloon from January 1937. (Birmingham Central Reference Library)

The Kalamazoo Co. was a breakaway firm set up on the Mill Lane site in Northfield in 1908 by Birmingham stationers Paul Impey and Oliver Morland. The original US-based company was based in Kalamazoo in Michigan and Impey and Morland expanded the loose-leaf binding manufacturing into binders, specialist wrappers and labels. The interwar factory was built on the floodplain of the river Rea, which was both bridged and forded by Mill Walk. In the background is the incredibly low bridge under the main-line Birmingham to Gloucester railway line and on the extreme left one of the Austin Village's pre-fabricated and imported American timber bungalows, built in 1917, is visible. A new, greatly enlarged factory was built in 1962 and as Kalamazoo-Reynolds the company now provides unique IT solutions. (Birmingham Central Reference Library)

The extension of the tram service to Longbridge on 17 December 1923 ensured that new housing both along and beyond Bristol Road South would quickly consume the farmland to the south of Northfield. Along with the associated local shops the next thing to be built was always the public house. Although planned in 1925, the huge new King George V roadhouse was not opened until 20 January 1937, exactly a year to the day after the King had died. It closed as a pub during the summer of 2002 and is now a Cantonese Restaurant. It is seen in March 1979 when Dutch Elm Disease necessitated the felling of all the elm trees on what had been the tram central reservation. (Birmingham Central Reference Library)

Jones' Industrial Café and Restaurant seems to be doing a good trade as customers are sitting at the outside tables. Behind the café is the Danilo cinema which was opened on 26 January 1938 and would be taken over in 1954 by and renamed Essoldo. 70hp tram 533 speeds away towards Northfield on 7 June 1952 as a Fordson 7W lorry heads towards Longbridge. This would be one of the trams stored on the reserved track in Bristol Road and would remain there for eighteen days before being driven to Witton depot for breaking up. (H.B. Priestley)

Dropping off passengers in Bristol Road South is car 808, one of the Brush totally enclosed Maley & Taunton air-brake cars built in 1928. On 25 May 1952 the tramcar is working on the 71 service to Rubery and is standing opposite the Austin West Works. This was completed in 1917 fronting Bristol Road South and the two-storey structure used a simple brick style influenced by the Arts and Crafts movement. The tram is standing at the end of the central reservation at the Longbridge Lane junction. (M.J. O'Connor)

Caught in the traffic waiting to cross the Longbridge Lane traffic lights in Longbridge, Guy 'Arab' IV 2959 (JOJ 959) is working on the 63 service in 1966. The bus has been fitted with one of BCT's own – quite awful – fibreglass radiator grills. Behind the bus is the West Works. Work on building the West Works started in December 1916 and was finished in June 1917. It was paid for by the Government in the First World War to produce mainly shells. Work on demolishing the site started in June 2006 and was completed by Christmas 2006. (R. Marshall)

Cresting the railway bridge over the Halesowen Joint branch line is an Austin A40 pickup truck which is passing the interwar entrance to Longbridge station. The station eventually closed on 6 January 1964 after a very anonymous existence, as it was never mentioned in any public timetables. In early July 1952, two Brush-bodied EMB bogie air brake cars – 807 and the following 810 – wait for the points to be moved so that they can turn right through the island into Bristol Road South on their way to Rubery. A section of redundant, low-retaining wall outside the main entrance to the Austin factory which had separated the trams from other traffic has already been taken down in preparation for the forthcoming abandonment. (W.A. Camwell)

The only tram junction on the Bristol Road was at Longbridge where the 71 service turned through the traffic island and travelled about one mile along the reserved track in Bristol Road South to the Rubery terminus. At the end of June 1952, making the right turn towards Rubery, is UEC-built bogie car 559. Austin car workers end their shift and run towards the distant waiting trams in Lickey Road. The two trams standing at the pair of large passenger shelters are 70hp UEC-built cars 517 and 528 which are dwarfed by Nazareth House. This Roman Catholic orphanage, emerging above the trees, was built in 1912 and later became a home for the elderly. (F.N. Lloyd Jones)

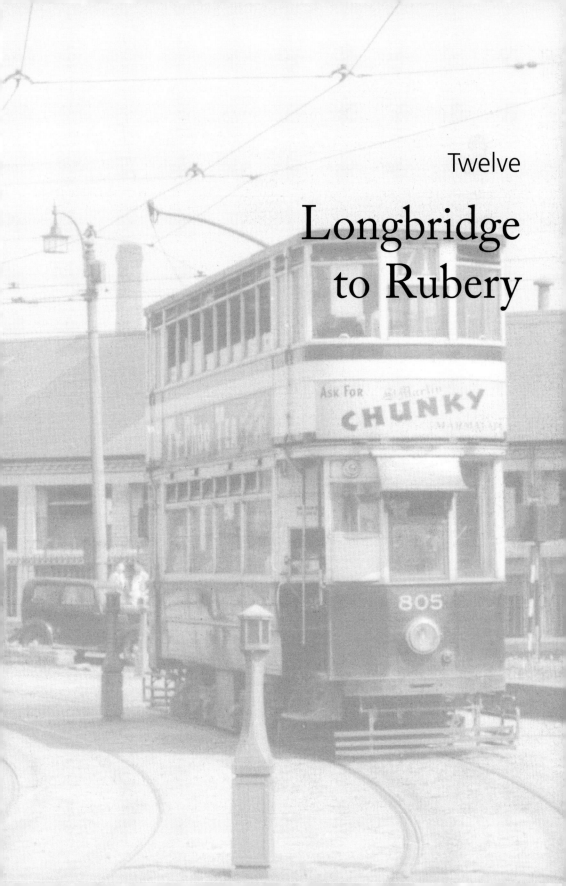

Twelve

Longbridge to Rubery

The Longbridge to Rubery service opened on Monday 8 February 1926 in order to serve the new municipal and private housing which was being built in the area in the mid-1920s. On its way to Rubery on the 71 route in July 1951, car 805, a 1928 EMB air-brake car built by Brush, negotiates the traffic island at the Longbridge junction. The driver of this tram has the sun shade extended as he drives towards the Rubery terminus on this sunny afternoon. Behind the tram is the original Austin office block of 1905, later known as the South Works. (A.W.V. Mace)

Totally enclosed, Brush-bodied EMB bogie car 746 climbs up the slight gradient in Bristol Road South as it travels away from the tramway junction at Longbridge towards the Rubery terminus. The tram is passing the row of interwar shops next to the junction with Cliff Rock Road when working on the 71 route in 1951. The Rubery reserved track route was opened on 8 February 1926, coincidentally the same year as the 732 class was introduced. This class of BCT tram was unique and could be easily identified as beneath the angled balcony windows were a pair of handrails used by the cleaning and maintenance staff to enable them to get onto the roof of the trams. (W.J. Wyse)

Car 752, a Brush totally enclosed, 63hp bogie car dating from 1926 has just left the Rubery terminus and is travelling along Bristol Road South towards Longbridge. It is working on the 71 route during August 1951. Just visible above the early 1930s semi-detached houses is the Longbridge public house. This large roadhouse had been opened as an M&B public house on 4 March 1932 and was demolished soon after, closing in December 1995 to make way for housing. (F.N. Lloyd Jones)

An MG TB sport saloon travels towards the city boundary at Rubery, passing rows of interwar semi-detached houses. Brush-bodied, EMB bogie 63hp car 780 sets out on the 71 service on the long journey to Birmingham. On the left is the wall surrounding the large, Corporation-owned Rubery Hill Mental Hospital. This isolated group of buildings was built in 1882 to relieve the overcrowding at the early Victorian inner-city Winson Green Hospital. It was able to accommodate about 820 long-term patients and was impressed in the First World War by the War Department as a hospital to treat severely wounded soldiers who were brought in by ambulance from the nearby Rubery station. (W.J. Wyse)

Soon after the opening of the Rubery tram route to its terminus at Leach Green Lane on 8 February 1926, car 305, an open-balconied four-wheeler dating from 1911, stands at the recently opened terminus. When this terminus was being constructed a lot of sandstone was excavated from the Leach Heath quarries at the bottom of Rednal Hill. This was partially in connection with the proposed tramway terminal loop built in the manner of the nearby Rednal terminus, but it was never completed. This left the trams at Rubery looking very lost in the centre of the wide open spaces for the next twenty-three years. Next to car 305 is the ornate tram shelter and beyond that is the steep climb of the still-rural Cock Hill Lane. Behind the tramcar are the Congregational chapel and the community hall dating from 1841 which both survived until they were burnt down in 1959. (Birmingham Central Reference Library)

Although it is 1943 and the tram is fitted with wartime headlight masks and white blackout paint, car 741, a seventeen-year-old Brush-bodied EMB air-brake 63hp bogie car, still looks well maintained despite the privations of the Second World War. It is standing at the terminus where a trough has been put above the overhead to mask any flashes as the conductor takes off or puts back the trolleypole. Behind the distant trees are the extensive grounds of Rubery Hill Mental Hospital. (Burrows Brothers)

On 24 May 1952, car 774, one of the Brush-built totally enclosed air-brake bogie cars which had spent from 1928 until 1950 working on the bow-collector routes operated by Washwood Heath depot, stands at the Rubery terminus in Bristol Road South. When the tram route was extended from Longbridge to Rubery on 8 February 1926, it became the fourth from last tramway extension to be opened in Birmingham. The grassy bank on the right is the edge of the 821ft Rednal Hill at the junction of Leach Green Lane. (H.V. Jinks)

Parked at the 63 route bus terminus in Bristol Road South is a Crossley-bodied Crossley DD42/6 2414 (JOJ 414) dating from June 1950. This was one of the batch of thirty Crossley HOE7/5B downdraught-engined buses and the last exposed radiator double-deckers to enter service in Birmingham. The Crossley is about eight years old but it still retains its original trafficators. Beyond the bus are the gates of the Rubery Hill Mental Hospital. (J. Carroll)

The twelve Ford R192s with Strachan B46F were the first 'lightweight' buses bought by the Corporation for use on the proposed network of Limited Stop Services which were to be introduced in the city. The Strachan body construction was somewhat flimsy but the undertaking did get a creditable ten-year service out of them. 3656 (JOL 656E) waits alongside the Rubery by-pass flyover at the terminus of the 99 route on 3 April 1967, the first day of operation. These buses had a livery of cream with only the skirt panels painted dark blue. They were fitted with non-standard, rather hard red covered, seats. (L. Mason)

The driver and conductor of the 1913 Daimler 40hp bus 7 (OA 1607) pose in front of their bus outside the New Rose & Crown in 1914. The terminus was outside the ivy-covered inn which had replaced the Old Rose & Crown at Rednal in 1831 when the new road was built avoiding the steep climb over the Lickey Hills. Its heyday as a coaching inn was short-lived once the Birmingham to Gloucester railway had been completed over the fearsome 1 in 37 incline of the famous Lickey Bank as far as Cofton Farm station on 17 December 1840. Through services to Birmingham commenced on 17 August 1841 and soon the old coaching inn became just a village pub. (D.R. Harvey collection)

Unlike the trams which succeeded the bus service, the Corporation-owned buses crossed the county boundary into Worcestershire and terminated in New Road, Rubery, on the forecourt of the New Rose & Crown. In early November 1913 the driver and conductor of 7 (OA 1607), a Daimler 40hp with a LGOC O18/16RO body, are standing with some of the Rubery 'locals' who have come to see the new buses. Behind the bus is the early Victorian Rubery Congregational chapel and the community hall. (D.R. Harvey collection)

Turning into Cock Hill Lane from Rubery Lane near to the Cock Inn is 3906 (SOE 906H). On 10 June 1972 the bus is about to pull up at the Bundy Clock which had been installed at this recently introduced terminus. 3906 is working on the 63 route which had been extended from the original terminus at Leach Green Lane in order to serve the first stage of the Frankley housing development. This bus was one of 100 Daimler 'Fleetline' CRG6LX/33s, fitted with Park Royal H47/33D bodywork, which were ordered by Birmingham City Transport but delivered to West Midlands Travel. (E.V. Trigg)

thirteen

Longbridge to Rednal and the Lickeys

Seen at Longbridge in early 1914 are at least six of the ten original buses which began bus operations by the then Birmingham Corporation Tramways Department. These Daimler CC-type buses had entered service on 19 July 1913 when the tramway feeder route from Selly Oak to Rednal was opened. The branch to Rubery was opened on 29 November 1913 and both routes served the rapidly expanding Austin Motor Works. The bus facing towards Rednal in Lickey Road is bus 5 (OA 1605) and like all the other buses has been fitted with windscreens. (J. Whybrow)

An early 1920s Austin 12/4 open tourer waits to turn into Bristol Road at the main entrance to the Austin Motor Co. factory. Herbert Austin left the Wolseley Co. and set up his car factory in 1905 in a disused factory which had formerly made colour-printed tin containers. By the 1920s, Longbridge had become the largest car factory in the world and during this period Austin became interested in manufacturing smaller vehicles, such as the tiny, revolutionary Austin 7. (Birmingham Central Reference Library)

In the 1920s and '30s the Austin Motor Works needed ninety-one trams at the end of the shifts to move the workforce when the total allocation of Selly Oak depot was only just over 100 trams. In about 1935, throngs of car workers, all wearing the mandatory cap, rush along Lickey Road to climb on to the waiting tramcars. All the motorcars appear to be Austins with the one on the right, a 10/4 model, being a new 1934 model. (Birmingham Central Reference Library)

The long row of shelters was for the inward-bound car workers, though the outbound passengers on trams going to Rednal did not have the same luxury. In about 1949, car 775, one of the fifty Brush-bodied, totally enclosed, bogie air-brake cars of 1928 has just deposited some passengers at the stop outside the main gates of the Austin factory. The tram is about to travel up Lickey Road towards the terminus at Rednal. In the distance is a tram turning into Bristol Road South on a 71 service to Rubery. (C. Carter)

As the man smoking the cigarette turns the page of his newspaper, bus 47 (OB 2101), an AEC Y-type, loads up with Austin workers in Lickey Road, Longbridge. The bus is working on the Rednal service in about 1919. The bus is still carrying its original Dodson O18/15RO body which it will retain for another three years. Such was the post-war need for transport that convertible lorries with benches and canvas tilt-tops were used to carry workers. An unidentifiable lorry-bus speeds up Lickey Road towards Redditch. (Birmingham Central Reference Library)

Car 805, a sixty-two-seat 63hp bogie car, built by Brush in 1928, passes the pre-fabs at the top of the climb up Lickey Road opposite Edgewood Road in the winter of 1951 when the leafless branches of the trees alongside the reserved track point starkly towards the sky. These supposedly temporary bungalows backed onto Cofton Park and managed to survive for about twenty years. Parked in front of the pre-fabs is a mid-1930s Morris Ten-Four saloon. The tram, which weighed 16¾ tons, is working on the usual 70 route and appears to be fairly full as it powers its way towards the Rednal terminus. (D. Gill)

As a Morris-Commercial CV ambulance, owned by the City of Birmingham, heads up the hill in Lickey Road on 18 July 1949 two trams are about to pass each other on the central reservation. Air-brake car 739 of 1926 is heading towards Longbridge while 70hp tram 531, originally built in 1913 with open balconies, is travelling towards the Rednal terminus. (D.R. Harvey collection)

The popularity of the Lickey Hills was such that even during the Second World War special trams were laid on to take parties to Rednal. With railway and motor coach excursions totally stopped for the duration, a trip to the Lickeys was often the only option. Operating on a Sunday School Special is one of Coventry Road depot's four-wheel, open-balconied, UEC-bodied trams. Car 383 is standing at the entrance to the terminus loop at the top of Lickey Road. (Burrows Brothers)

This is what it was like during every summer weekend since the route extension to Rednal was opened in 1924. Only this was 24 May 1952 and the days of thirty trams parked around the terminus loop were numbered! The journey to Rednal on long sections of reserved track was 8.19 miles from the City terminus in Navigation Street. Although the standard Birmingham bogie tramcar did not look particularly modern, their electrics, brakes and motors underneath were as up-to-date with contemporary tramway practice as any other system in the UK. On the right car 765 is parked in the siding at the front of the tram shelters as there is no room around the gardens. (H.V. Jinks)

The impressive tram shelters at Rednal were built in 1925 at the same time as the ornamental gardens and the loop. After the extension had been opened on 14 April 1924, the trams initially terminated at Leach Green Lane, though this was soon moved to a stub opposite the Hare & Hounds public house. Car 756 was one of the last seven of these first air-brake trams in the Birmingham fleet which spent their entire lives working on the Bristol Road services. (A. Yates)

During the summer of 1914 one of Birmingham Corporation Tramway's first double-deckers, 2 (OA 1602), a Daimler 40hp with an LGOC O18/16RO body, stands at the terminus of the Rednal. The Hare and Hounds public house had been substantially rebuilt in the Edwardian period with a mock-Tudor frontage. At this time this pub was one of four in Lickey Road providing refreshment for the visitors to the Lickey Hills. (Birmingham Central Reference Library)

By September 2007 a much-extended Old Hare & Hounds public house still attracts a lot of business, although like the whole of the Rednal area it could no longer be regarded as a tourist attraction. The public house has lost most of its Tudor trimmings and has been considerably enlarged in order to accommodate a restaurant. The hostelry overlooks a small 1980s housing estate site which was built on part of the old tramway turning circle. (D.R. Harvey)

The 1924 extension to Rednal was operated from Bournbrook depot until Selly Oak depot opened three years later. It would be another year before the terminus loop was available and the ornamental gardens were laid out. Four-wheeled UEC open balcony car 349 stands at the terminus in the summer of 1924 when the passenger shelters were yet to be constructed and the shops and cafés opposite the new tram terminus were yet to be built. The tram is displaying a side slip board which is showing REDNAL 70. (D.R. Harvey collection)

It is 18 July 1949 as Brush totally enclosed air-brake car 739 waits at the end of the tram shelters with the perimeter of the ornamental gardens in the foreground. The tram is still painted in the pre-war livery with full lining-out and cream rocker panels. The end of the shelters and the position of the Bundy clock was the length of a tram, about 33ft 6in long, which enabled passengers to get onto the tram at the nearside rear platform while the driver could just dismount and peg the clock from the front of the tram. (C.C. Thornburn collection)

In September 2007, little of the old attractions and buildings still survive in Rednal, although this little wooden shop, used for many years as an ice cream store, was still clinging on, albeit in a derelict condition. This sad remnant of the gentler post-First World War days reminds one of walks through the Lickey Hills, cafés, tearooms and amusement arcades. This was when the Quaker ideals of the Cadbury family, who bought and then donated the Lickey Hills to Birmingham Corporation for use by the citizens of Birmingham, really made a day out a treat for the hard-pressed industrial workers' families. (D.R. Harvey)

In August 1939 an immaculate-looking car, 590, stands at the end of the impressive curve of cast-iron and glass shelters at the Rednal terminus loop. The conductor stands talking to the tram driver with his back to the Bundy timekeeping clock. Car 590 was a Brush-bodied, re-motored 63hp car mounted on Brush maximum traction bogies. This type of bogie had 31¾in-diameter wheels on the two outer axles which carried about 80 per cent of the tram's weight. A smaller set of 21¾in inner wheels helped to guide the tram and provide extra stability. The journey from Rednal took about 50 minutes and still only cost 5d. (E.W. Dash)

Rednal was the gateway to the 950ft-high Lickey Hills which formed part of a ridge from the Clent Hills in the south to Sedgley Beacon, which is part of the main watershed in England. On high-days and holidays during the late 1920s and '30s, the extra traffic generated by the attractions at the Lickey Hills was phenomenal. On 28 June 1952, just one week before the abandonment, UEC-built 70hp bogie car 533 stands alongside the toilet block located next to the turning loop having just arrived in Rednal. (H. Sargeant, Birmingham Central Reference Library collection)

Opposite above: The wooded Bilberry Hill looks down over the Rednal terminus in the summer of 1951. Car 738, one of the air-braked Brush bogie cars of 1926, stands alongside the last of the wrought-iron tram shelters and waits for the next group of passengers to travel back to the city centre. The three hills to the east, Rednal, Bilberry and Cofton, form the Lickey Ridge and are made up of Lickey quartzite. This is a 570-million-year-old Cambrian structure and unlike most quartzites it is a sedimentary, rather than metamorphic, rock. (D.A. Jones)

Opposite below: A good sample of the buses allocated to Selly Oak garage in the mid-1950s stand on the abandoned tram tracks at the Rednal 62 bus terminus. 2953 (JOJ 953), a 1952 Guy 'Arab' IV, with a 27ft-long MCCW H30/25R body, is parked alongside the railings while alongside it is 1951-vintage 2608 (JOJ 608), another Guy 'Arab' but this time a 26ft-long Mark III Special, also bodied by Metro-Cammell. Drawn up behind 2953 is an exposed radiator Crossley DD42/6 with a Crossley H30/24R body. (C. Carter)

Some thirteen years later, the Guy 'Arab' IVs were still hard at work on the Bristol Road services, including the 62 route to Rednal. 2959 (JOJ 959), by now with its front wings cut back in order to get more air onto the fade-prone brakes of the Guy, has been fitted with one of the anonymous BCT-designed fibre-glass radiator grills. On the right is Park Royal-bodied Daimler 'Fleetline' CRG6LX 3759 (KOX 759F) which had recently entered service on 23 February 1968. (L. Mason)

There can't be many structures which have been a public convenience, a tourist information office, a local transport history museum and tea rooms and a Chinese restaurant. Yet the building alongside the preserved short stretch of tram tracks, which is just visible in the gap in the hedge next to the telegraph pole, at the old Rednal tram terminus, has been all of these! On 23 September 2007 it was the Lailing Cantonese Restaurant. (D.R. Harvey)

On 23 September 2007, the long-abandoned tram tracks alongside the Lailing Restaurant at the old Rednal tram terminus are just visible under the weeds. It is a long time since that first summer after the end of the First World War, when over 20,000 people a day went to visit the Lickeys; this was five years before the trams arrived and crowds stretched as far as the golf course in Rose Hill. After the Bristol Road trams were abandoned, a section of the terminus loop survived for

many years. Latterly the tracks were preserved as a reminder of a tram journey to the Lickeys, though recently a spot of weed killer and a bit of TLC wouldn't come amiss. (D.R. Harvey)

Journey's end! This is what the Brummies wanted when, during the inter-war period, they crowded onto the Rednal trams and went for a day trip to 'The Lickeys'. The Cofton Wood tea rooms, country hostelries and public houses such as the Hare & Hounds at Rednal, the fairgrounds, and walks through the woods and open parkland were great attractions. Beacon Hill is composed of 280-million-year-old Permian Clent Breccia, which is compacted gravel, consisting of reddish angular rock fragments surrounded by large amounts of muddy rock. It was formed as a flash flood deposit, laid down in a hot desert by short-lived torrential streams. The present-day landscaped river Arrow valley with its waterfalls, wooden bridges and ornamental gardens, as well as the revered 1890 grave of Cardinal Newman in the grounds near the Oratory Retreat House, were further attractions at the Lickey Hills. All this for a 5d tramcar ride! (Birmingham Central Reference Library)

This is why people in their thousands went to the Lickeys by tram and, for a much shorter time, by bus: the approach to the Lickey Hills viewed from Groveley Lane with the wooded Rednal Hill on the right and Beacon Hill in the distance. (Birmingham Central Reference Library)

Opposite above: Looking down from Bilberry Hill, near to the tea rooms, across to the distant Beacon Hill, the Rose & Crown nestles at the bottom of Rose Hill alongside the upper course of the river Arrow. Rose Hill was part of the original road to Bristol but was too steep for the stage coaches. This is why a new, easier route was cut through Rubery to Longbridge in 1831. On the site there had been a coaching inn but this was replaced in 1880 by the present Old Rose & Crown building. In 1904, J.R.R. Tolkien, author of *The Hobbit*, moved to Rednal with his mother, who was convalescing. The hills became a favourite haunt for him and are the inspiration for the mythical Shires where the hobbits lived in his book. (Birmingham Central Reference Library)

Opposite below: Nestling beneath Beacon Hill, the Rose & Crown has survived as a public house and a function centre. On 23 September 2007 the hotel looked in excellent condition. The Lickey Hills Country Park has been a country park since 1971 and is 212ha in area. It has hilltops, woodlands, conifer plantations and heathland, an excellent visitor centre and signed trails across the hills. Recreational use dates from 1888 and after the city finally purchased Cofton Hill, Lickey Warren and Pinfield Wood in 1920, the Cadbury family purchased the Rose Hill Estate in 1923, thus assuring free public access to the hills. (D.R. Harvey)

Other local titles published by The History Press

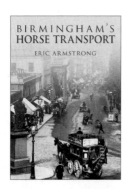

Birmingham's Horse Transport
ERIC ARMSTRONG

Eric Armstrong takes us on a tour of the city using images of horses at work; from the city centre to the northern suburbs (Handsworth, Perry Barr, Aston and Erdington), and the southern suburbs (Moseley, Edgbaston, Saltley, Bournville), this book provides an invaluable record of the contribution made by horses to the city's welfare.

978 0 7524 4613 4

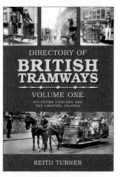

Title Sub-title
AUTHOR

As trams and other light rapid transit systems make a comeback in many British cities, this volume, the first of three, looks at all the tramways that have operated in the towns and cities of southern England and the Channel Islands. From the 1870s to the 1950s, trams were a common sight in many British towns. From the pioneering Oystermouth Tramroad of 1807 to the up-to-the-minute systems of Nottingham and Dublin of 2004, this is the definitive directory of the tramway lines and networks of the British Isles.

978 0 7524 3901 3

Red Rover Bus Company
ROBERT COOK

The Red Rover story began with the Cain brothers in pre-war London before they moved base to Aylesbury following the nationalisation of the company's express coach and local services. The company was taken over by Keith Garages in 1955, becoming a sister company to Keith Coaches. The story more or less ended in 1987, following de-regulation of bus and coach services. Robert Cook tells the story of Red Rover from its formation to its disappearance.

978 0 7524 4442 0

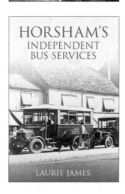

Horsham's Independent Bus Services
LAURIE JAMES

This book outlines the history of the independent bus services that have run in Horsham and the nearby area from the early 1920s until the present day. The author sets out to capture the entrepreneurial spirit of the early operators who brought new-found mobility to rural folk. Illustrated with over 150 images, many previously unpublished, the book will be of interest to both locals and enthusiasts alike.

978 0 7524 4444 1

If you are interested in purchasing other books published by The History Press, or in case you have difficulty finding any History Press books in your local bookshop, you can also place orders directly through our website
www.thehistorypress.co.uk